SMALLWAR

MY TWENTY-SEVEN MONTHS AS
A MEDIC IN VIETNAM

LARRY KIPP

D1596995

HELLGATE PRESS   ASHLAND, OR

SMALLWAR

Published by Hellgate Press

(An imprint of L&R Publishing, LLC)

Hellgate Press

PO Box 3531

Ashland, OR 97520

email: sales@hellgatepress.com

Interior Design: Sasha Kincaid Cover

Design: L. Redding

Photos of Larry Kipp taken by Crew Chief Tom Cash. Used with permission.

ISBN: 978-1-954163-42-3

Printed and bound in the United States of America

First edition 10 9 8 7 6 5 4 3 2 1

Dedicated to all those we couldn't save

FOREWORD

SMALLWAR BY LARRY KIPP IS A MUST-READ PUBLICATION for veterans or others interested in learning about a soldier's experiences in Vietnam. Larry's stories are brief, for the most part, and give the reader a quick insight to his personal and unique experiences pre-through post-Vietnam. For a big man, over 200 pounds, I found Larry to be one of the more intellectual and sensitive people with whom I f lew combat missions in an ugly war.

Larry covers the medic's role flying unarmed medical evacuation helicopters, Dustoff. He shares, with openness, the errors he made as a new crewmember and with humbleness shares how he and his peers saved countless lives with rudimentary medical tools available to them. Hundreds of missions flown, hundreds of patient's lives saved only to rejected by his non-combat peers when he returns to the States. After nearly 50 years, he and his son return to Vietnam to seek out the beauty he found during his combat tour from late 1967 to 1970. A mission of healing and reconnecting with the soul of a gentle man.

He searched for Love—found it and was rejected by it. In his stories you sense the pain inflected by this rejection. A soldier in Vietnam on a 3 day in-country pass or R&R or a 7 day out of country leave or R&R have several things on their mind— sex, booze, good food and relaxation. Larry takes a belated in-country R&R and hangs out with the Nguyen's. Larry skips those four R&R "objectives" and adds a fifth one—genuine human interaction with the indigenous population. He shares those insights with the reader, and you begin to understand why this "gentle giant" is drawn to people for who they are. This intellect and gentleness may be the reason he became a biologist with an interest in Orchids.

Borneo is a destination of adventure for one of his out of country trips. Borneo is not an "approved" DoD destinations for soldier R&Rs nor one that would be attractive to a soldier looking for a reprieve from the rigors of jungle combat. He shares how and why he went to Borneo and partied with former head-hunters. Did Larry find love in Borneo? He will explain how "botanizing" caused a temporary loss of situational awareness while still finding his way back to the combat zone.

We can all learn lessons from this book and from Larry's insight.

Steve Vermillion
Lieutenant Colonel (Retired), US Army
Call Sign: "Dustoff 40" - 1969

"Small wars are always teetering on the brink of becoming big ones."

-Max Lerner

CONTENTS

A helicopter ambulance (HA), also known as a Medevac, but known to Vets by its call sign: Dustoff. Image courtesy of The Dustoff Association (https://www. facebook.com/TheDustoffAssociation)

AUTHOR'SNOTE:

ACOLLECTIONOFMEMORIESFROMTHE AUTHOR'SPERSONALRECORDS

WELL, IT'S TIME TO WRITE DOWN WHAT I remember about Vietnam and Army life, and the Vietnam Veterans Against the War, our family arguments regarding the Nam policy, and all that, in no particular order. I'm calling this collection of stories Smallwar, in honor of a quotation by Max Lerner: "Small wars are always teetering on the brink of becoming big ones." —1978

I just want to jot some things down that will serve to jog my memory. But, before that, I just want to say that this collection of remembrances are just tiny vignettes of the life I have lived in the military.

I am not morally superior. I am not hurt more than the average GI who went to 'Nam. I am nothing special. In less than 50 years, I'll be dust . . . like so many soldiers who went to war before me. But I hope these small remembrances may live on a bit longer.

I especially want my son to read these . . . not so much to understand anything in particular . . . but to share with him a part of me that existed long before he was born. Perhaps, if I really finish this, he may pass these "war stories" on to his children. —1987

I want to thank my son, Mastin, for urging me to take him to Vietnam and show him the "two good things I saw" over there during the war. Sadly, only one of them remains. Our three- hour visit with the Buddhist monk in Da Lat has served me well since.

It took a while, but since my return to the States, I now find myself emotionally removed from that time and place. The emotions still exist, but they have become occupants and not drivers of my thoughts.

I now know the war is over, both over there, and in here, in my head. But the memories never leave. —2017

Intellectually, I know the war is over, but while writing this I reopened old memories, almost forgotten. First a trickle, then a flood. I haven't slept well since, until I started taking CBD daily. Sleep is improved, but there is no daily cycle yet. And still, the memories keep coming. —2019

Larry Kipp (Photo by Crew Chief Tom Cash)

MILITARY ABBREVIATIONS AND DEFINITIONS

25-Hour Inspection: Choppers were required to have 25-hour, 50-hour, and 100hour inspections. Each one was different, more intense. Upon reaching the 50th f light hour, we had to pull a 25-hour and a 50- hour inspection, and so on. (All flight hours and inspections were logged into the Crew Chief's log book.)

A&D: Admissions and Dispositions

AC: Aircraft Commander

AGL: above ground level

AIT: Advanced Individual Training, after Basic training

AO: Area of Operations; also Agent Orange

ARVN: Army of the Republic of Vietnam, also known as the South Vietnamese Army (SVA)

BASIC: Basic training in the military. Here you are taught how to dress, act, and march as a soldier, and how to train to be a warrior.

Bn: Battalion

Bolt holes: bunkers

Brown Water NAVY: A combination of U.S. Navy, Coast Guard, and U.S. Army armed patrol boats securing the river passages of the Mekong Delta. Navy ships that served at sea were the "Blue Water Navy."

CIB: Combat Infantryman's Badge

CO: Commanding Officer

DEROS: Date Eligible for Return from Overseas

DI: Drill Instructor

DMZ: demilitarized zone

DOD: Department of Defense

Dustoff(s): The call sign for an unarmed medevac helicopter serving in Vietnam; also known as a HA (helicopter ambulance). The term was assigned by the Navy (responsible for all call signs in Vietnam) to Major Lloyd E. Spencer, Commander of the U. S. Army 57th Medical Detachment (HA) for use as his units medevacs. Call signs were normally replaced every few months but Maj. Spencer petitioned to keep the call sign permanently for all unarmed HAs controlled by the 44th Medical Brigade in Vietnam.

EM: Enlisted Men

ER: Emergency Room

FNG: Fucking New Guy

FSB: Fire Support Base

GI: Initials used to describe soldiers of the US Army. (One theory is that initially

G.I. stood for Galvanized Iron, then Government Issue or General Issue, and some soldiers began referring to themselves as GI, or GI Joe, to symbolize they were mass-produced products of the government.)

GRS: Graves Registration Service

GWS: The Geneva Convention for the Amelioration of the Condition of the Wounded and Sick in Armed Forces in the Field

HA: Helicopter Ambulance; see Dustoff

Hooch: Any living quarters. Also spelled hootch.

IED: improvised explosive device, also a mine or booby trap

IG: Inspector General

KIA: Killed in Action

Klick: Also spelled click, is slang for kilometer.

LRRP: Long Range Recon Patrol, pronounced "lerps"

LST: Landing Ship Tank

LTC: Lieutenant Colonel

LZ: Landing Zone; a hot LZ is a Landing Zone taking fire

MACV: Military Assistance Command Vietnam

MIKE FORCES: Mobile Strike Forces formed of Montagnards and Cambodian irregulars and organized by the Special Forces

MOH: Medal of Honor

Montagnards: Indigenous people of the Central Highlands of Vietnam. The term "Montagnard" means "people of the mountain" in French and is a carryover from the French colonial period in Vietnam. Also called The Degar and Nung.

MOS: Military Occupational Specialty

MPC: Army money

NCOIC: Non-Commissioned Officer in Charge

NG: National Guard

NVA: North Vietnamese Army

OJT: On-the-job training

PSP: perforated steel plating, otherwise known as a Marston Mat, used in the creation of runways.

R&R: Rest and Recreation

Real World: To all U.S. soldiers serving in Vietnam, back home was the Real World.

Ringer's Solution: A solution of several salts dissolved in water for the purpose of creating an isotonic solution relative to the body fluids of the patient.

RTO: Radio Telephone Operator

RVN: Republic of Vietnam

Sapper: VC who would sneak into the bases with explosives

SGM: Sergeant Major

Short Timers: Those with less than 100 days left In Country

SOCOM: Special Operations Command

SOP: Standard Operating Procedure

STOL: short takeoff and landing

STRAC: Strategic Army Corps meaning in tip-top shape, ready to go.

SVA: South Vietnamese Army; see ARVN

TDY: Temporary duty

TOE: Table of Operations and Equipment

Triple S'd: Shit, shower, shave

VC: Viet Cong (local rebels) or, shorter version "Charlie" since the radio phonetic of VC is Victor Charlie

WAC: Women's Army Corps

WIA: Wounded in Action

WO: Warrant Officer

xO: Executive Officer

INTRODUCTION
EARLY LIFE LESSONS

SINCE WHEN I WAS VERY YOUNG, ANYTIME I saw trouble, I wanted to help. That didn't mean I knew how to help, but that didn't matter. I tried anyway. My parents' guidance and life's lessons would eventually show me the way, but that's not in this story.

My earliest recollection of trying to help was in second grade at Oak Grove Elementary School, in Elsmere, Delaware, an old, beautiful brick building which has since been occupied by the city police department. It was 1955, I was seven years old and it was a beautiful spring day. As recess ended, we lined up to go inside. Two boys I didn't know were next to me and they got into a pushing match. Without thinking, I stepped in and pushed them away from each other. At that moment, a teacher I didn't know heard the ruckus and turned to see what was going on.

Simultaneously, one of the boys I pushed had spun and his face went into the corner of the brick building. The teacher singled me out and told me to "go to the Principal's Office."

Knowing I did nothing wrong, I went in the building and walked down the hall to the office. The office was in the center of the building with no windows, just a window above. To enter the office, you had to walk through a smaller room where they kept office supplies. As I walked into that room for the first time, I saw a cylindrical machine with a handle on it, attached to a long board. *This must be the spanking machine I had heard the third-graders talking about,* I thought.

I got scared. I didn't deserve to get spanked, especially by a machine. That wasn't right. I turned around and walked out of the building, across the now empty playground, and walked the two miles to my home in Willow Run. When I walked past a marvelous rose garden, I stopped to smell one of the first roses of spring. Years later, I would learn it was a Peace Rose, and it smelled wonderful. As I walked into the house, my mother saw me and asked what I was doing home so early.

I hadn't thought about what I was going to tell her, and I immediately lied. "They sent me home because I am sick." Mom hugged me and put me in bed, then made me some tomato soup and brought it to my room. I felt warm, cozy, and safe.

Some hours later, my dad arrived home from work and he and Mom talked. Then Dad came in and asked how I felt. I told him I was better, and he then said, "Mom told me the school called and they said you were not sick but were sent to the Principal's Office for bullying another boy."

Knowing that wasn't exactly right, I objected, but without artful articulation. My dad never yelled, or even raised his voice. He simply broke the accusation down into its single parts:

Did I push a boy?

"Yes, but after he had started it."

Did the boy I pushed hit the corner of the brick wall? "Yes."

Was I sent to the Principal's Office? "Yes," and I did go home instead? "Yes."

I told Dad about the spanking machine and how terrified I was of it and he said he would look into that, but, "Right now, you need to be punished for lying to Mom." Oh no! I did lie to Mom! It was my first lie and I felt ashamed and knew what was next. Dad removed his belt, I leaned over his knee, and he whacked me two times with the belt. Looking back on it, I realize they were not major "whacks," just enough to let me know I had done something wrong. I cried like a baby, out of humiliation, not pain.

A few days later, when we sat down for dinner, Dad told me he'd looked into the *spanking machine*. "It does look formidable, but it's really a printing press called a mimeograph machine," he said. We then discussed what a mimeograph machine was, and I realized all was forgiven.

The lessons I learned that day were several. First, never lie to Mom. Second, don't believe everything third-graders tell you. And third, don't jump to conclusions about what a machine you don't recognize does.

I also got a lesson from Dad about how to approach problems. At that age, I couldn't articulate it, but by the time I was a teen, I knew it was a good thing to break problems down into their individual parts and go from there. This was my first step in that direction.

Afterwards, that teacher still thought I was a bully, but I wasn't. I was just trying to do the right thing.

1   WHO AM I? WHO ARE YOU?

DURING LUNCH BREAK IN TWELFTH GRADE, A BRIGHT, pensive friend asked a philosophical question: "Who am I? Who are you?" It was that guy's nature to ask that question rhetorically, usually every day.

I thought for a moment, then said, "We won't know the answer to that until we've finished our lives. Only then, looking back on each choice we made, will we have defined ourselves. *That* will be 'who we are'." My answer had just popped out, startling even me.

My friend looked down at the floor for a moment, then turned and left without a word. I haven't changed my mind in all the years since that day. In fact, it has served as the foundation upon which I relied when faced with tough choices, even when I ended up choosing wrongly.

But the question did give me cause to consider my teenaged existence. I concluded I had never done anything important in my life. Further, the only benefit I brought to the world was that I breathed and consumed air, thereby providing the plants with some needed CO_2. Beyond that, my impact on the world was zero. *When I die,* I thought, *the world will not have noticed me.*

I considered most of my classmates in high school frivolous, since they never seemed to probe the mysteries of life beyond who might deign to go out with them to the hop on Saturday night. In our own way, I suppose, we all searched for true love—at least the songs on the AM radio said we did.

The year before (1963–1964), my folks had sent me to Fork Union Military Academy for my Junior year, hoping I'd raise my grades and avoid any more detentions. There, for the first time since second grade, I made the Honor Roll, since there was nothing to do at Fork Union but study. My mom was thrilled. I don't know how my Dad felt; he never talked much about his feelings.

But one year at Fork Union was enough. Too much was happening *on the outside.* President John F. Kennedy had been killed. Some group called the Beatles let the hair on the front of their heads hang down to their eyebrows. Plus, I'd had enough of the Spartan life.

The summer before my Senior year, I worked on the Goldwater campaign, manning a local office, on some of the afternoons. Politics, History, and Religion were the main topics at dinner each night, along with what happened that day. I'd picked up smoking at the military academy, settling on Pall Malls. I smoked a pack a day.

What I remember most about that election was:

- I got to drink my first beer at a conservative party (it was awful!);
- I learned to drive a stick shift at a farm;
- We lost the election; and
- After Goldwater lost to Lyndon Johnson, one of the big politicos went around selling gold "27" pins, because "27 million voters can't be wrong."

* * * * * *

My senior year, I returned to Brandywine High School, more confident about classes, and about myself. That school year (September 1964–June 1965) was magnificent. Classes were okay. Somehow girls found me attractive, though I didn't have a clue as to why, but I liked it. I wrestled on the Varsity team that year again, and came in third in the state. (Delaware is a small state).

I fell in love twice that year. First, with a foreign-exchange student from Norway named Astrid. Oh, what a sweetie. It may have been our joint emotional illiteracy, or the language barrier, or something else, but I was head-over-heels in love. That lasted about three months.

Around Christmas, something happened. I never did figure out what, but she seemed more distant. Like a clam, I closed myself up and tried to ignore her the rest of the year, though inside I ached for her. That March, I met Kathy, who was a junior. This relationship seemed to catch on, and by the time of the Senior Prom at the Hotel du Pont in Wilmington, on a warm, moist evening, I was hopelessly in love. For a while, life was wonderful.

I had to go to summer school in Ottawa, Kansas, to prove to the admissions committee at Ottawa University that I was, indeed, worthy of admission to the regular school year beginning in the Fall. What I mainly learned that summer was how many 15-cent schooners of 3.2 beer it took to get me really drunk. (There was no wine, no 6-percent beer, or any hard alcoholic beverages available in Kansas; too many people made money selling the 'Shine.) Since I hadn't had any alcohol since the election party the year before, it was like trying it for the first time all over again. Oh, that first beer! How awful it tasted. And, of course, it was a Budweiser.

While I was in Kansas, Kathy was back in Delaware. We wrote a lot, and those letters sustained me until I was able to return for a short while before Fall classes began. We renewed our friendship with abandon, well, almost. I fondly remember one night when I borrowed Dad's white Mercury and we saw a movie, before going parking over by Centerville. We made out passionately, for religious Christians. Without ever taking off a stitch of clothing or doing anything more than passionate kissing, we somehow were able to rehearse, emotionally, the rise, cresting, and fall of passion into a satiated state . . . when we simply hugged each other in a calm, contented way, listening to the Rock-n-Roll station, WAMS AM radio. We both fell asleep and woke much later to the tune of "Wake Up Little Susie." It was 3:45 AM, long after the 1 AM curfew, and I nearly jumped into a panic as I whisked my truelove home. Only later did I have time to smile at the irony of the music.

Soon, I was off to college and Kathy was now a senior in high school. Weekly letters sustained us both. I came home for Thanksgiving and Christmas, and all was well. Our Spring breaks didn't coincide—I was off a week earlier than her—so when I came back, she was still in classes. I wanted to surprise her by showing up in school and sneaking up behind her. Just before I did, I saw a guy come up to her and kiss her. To my surprise, she kissed him back! I went home confused and waited until school was over. Then I called and asked if it was okay to come over. "Of course!" is what I heard. So I did.

We were reacquainting ourselves inside when she went to answer a knock at the door. I am a patient fellow, sometimes. But after an hour, I went to the door and looked through the door window, and saw her sitting on the front step with that guy who kissed her at school. I waited another forty-five minutes until her older sister came to me and said how very sorry she was at how Kathy was behaving.

It was almost dinnertime by then, but they were occupying the front step. I didn't know how to leave. I was mortified at the thought of opening the door and asking them to move so I could leave. Instead, I went out the back way and walked between the houses, then to the car. A quick glance showed her looking at him, not me.

They watched me get into my car and drive away. I was ready to die and was too embarrassed to ever say anything. Thus ended my first real relationship.

It took me a while to get over this, but I eventually learned a general lesson: better *she* dumps me now than later. What she did, not how she did it, was a favor to me, in the long run.

I went back to Ottawa and was doing absolutely horribly. I was far more interested in honing my social skills than my intellectual ones. Besides, the classes were easy. I did discover that attendance mattered more than learning.

I took a political science course at 8:20 AM, Monday, Wednesday, and Fridays. I lived in a dorm on campus and it was a five-minute walk to the classroom. One morning, I woke up at my usual 8:00 AM and showered. I was fully soaped down when the water pressure died. *Oh no!*

The city had started their water main repairs. I already had three late calls in class; one more and I would get an automatic F!

I used the water in the toilet reservoir to get most of the soap off and ran to class—too late. Professor Averill chastised me in front of the class for being late one too many times and dismissed me. I stayed anyway, which greatly annoyed the professor. I went to the small discussion classes and took the quizzes, too.

When I showed up for the final, the professor asked in a squeaky voice loud enough for everyone to hear, "Why are you taking this? You already flunked the course." To which I replied, with very real anger, "Sir, some of us come here to learn, not just to get a grade." My moral indignation belied the fact that most of the semester I had simply goofed off, since the material came so easily to me.

Well, I got an A on the final, giving me a B average for the semester, but I took an F on the official transcript. This proved to me that "official records" don't always speak the truth.

2 SUMMER OF '66

THE SUMMER OF '66 WAS AMAZING. THERE WERE girls everywhere. I dated a succession of girls, all nifty and cute, but hormones ruled my courting. With all the passionate make-outs, not once that summer did anything close to friendship develop.

I got a job weeding at Phillip's Nursery in Wilmington at $1.12 per hour. This was far superior to the 60¢ an hour I made working for the ARA cafeteria at Ottawa, cleaning trays at lunch and dinner. Then, quite suddenly, several of us were laid off because there was no more weeding to do. I necessarily hitch-hiked to and from work, and this day was a somber one. I decided I had been economically murdered.

On that day, at the corner of Shipley and Wilson Road, I was picked up by a man named Bill, in a black Ford F10 pick-up truck. As we talked, I told him my troubles as he drove toward my home. By the end of the trip, Bill hired me to work for his new steel erection company, Falcon Steel, at the unheard-of wage of $1.50 per hour! I was in the bucks now!

Bill was a great taskmaster, a gruff appearing man, always busy with renting cranes, ensuring there were enough bolts, and looking over blueprints. One late afternoon, after work, I drove the F10 assigned to me by Bill to his home to get some orders. He invited me into his home in Green Meadow, not far from where Joe Biden lived. Our conversation ranged all over the place and finally settled on American writers; he brought out some writing he had done and read some of it to me. It was much in the spirit of Jack London. I was deeply touched by seeing this very human side of my master, the boss of fourteen burley ironworkers, as he read to me.

* * * * * *

That fall, at Ottawa, I met Theresa, among others. I realized at this time that I was about to flunk out of college, and I was kind of aware that there was a war going on somewhere, though no one at school ever talked about that. As a sophomore at Ottawa, I had declared my intellectual capacity by subscribing to *Time Magazine*, and they sometimes had a picture on the cover about this military thing in Vietnam. But it was far away, remote, not a part of my life.

I stayed in Ottawa that Thanksgiving, since it would have been a 1,200-mile drive to get home. Because it was a holiday, the university cafeteria was closed on Thursday until Monday, and I had to find some meals. I was broke, except for some 12-gage shotgun shells and a box of .22 rounds. I also had my Dad's .22 single shot rifle dated 1922, and I had hunted on and off during the Fall.

That Thanksgiving I borrowed a shotgun from my landlady, who had always cooked all my catches. I really liked the walks and views nearby, and I soon discovered squirrel is okay, but it took more to get full than I was ever to get in a day. Rabbit was the best, but you can only eat rabbit after the first hard frost. I hunted that holiday weekend and ate a lot of squirrel and one rabbit. But I got through the holiday.

It was a long, lonely weekend; it gave me pause to realize how lonely I was, how much of a failure I was in school, and how I had let down everyone who loved me, especially my Dad who had (so Mom told me) borrowed money for my tuition. Just like I had been let down by the one I loved. The blues flooded me and I sought solace from "Chewy," the nickname I had given to Theresa, in honor of the song "Chewy, Chewy," by Ohio Express, which had come out in the late 1960s.

Christmas came and went. The semester was to end at the end of January, and for once I had time to think about what I would do next. All my life I had been told what to do. Choosing had never been part of my experience, and something I had never considered, until now. I had a premonition that I would get drafted, go to Vietnam, and die. Here I was, eighteen years old, and I had never made love and felt as insignificant as if I had never been born. I didn't have a clue what sex was like, but I couldn't die without knowing.

One late January day, after mailing a bunch of letters to small newspapers, asking to be their war correspondent in Vietnam, and after applying for a passport, I took Chewy out to the woods, with a picnic lunch of hot dogs, buns, mustard, and sodas.

We ate, and we made love; we both wanted to. In the end, it was *coitus interruptus*, as I didn't want to make her pregnant.

Finally, my Bible reading had paid off. Someone in the Old Testament did that, and didn't get into too much trouble with God. But afterward, I was so embarrassed I took a walk to give Chewy time to clean up. I loved her, or thought I did, but I was aloof too, and I didn't know why. We both knew her dad, who was a pastor, would have never permitted us to date long-term, much less get married.

During this time, my brother Les and I became close. He was going to Drake University, doing a double major in History and Political Science. Boy, was I impressed. Earlier that summer, he had given me a great piece of advice: "It's okay to go to the limit, but do not exceed it." Then a discussion ensued focusing on how to know what your limit is. I have pondered that, on and off, ever since, with no satisfactory answer except to listen to your intuition, especially when you are in new territory. My conclusion thus far is: Success is what happens to you if you survive, and learn, from all your mistakes.

That cold weekend in January, I hitchhiked the 247 miles to Des Moines to see my brother. We went to a very confusing party; everyone was seemingly very friendly, but just as a conversation was getting interesting, whoever I was talking to left to go "discuss" something really important with someone else in the bathroom, the closet, the porch, or the attic. Only later did I realize they went off to smoke pot, which, at that point, I didn't know much about.

That night I slept on a couch in a two-room suite. I dreamt of Chewy, and making love to her, and I awoke in climax, only to realize that somehow I was still feeling as if I were still inside her. There was another person there with me. I froze to assess any danger I might be in. Then, the presence left me and moved to my friend's room. I heard whispering. "John! John! Wanna blow job?"

John replied, "By whom?"

Once he realized it was a guy, John walked him out of the house. I had been raped in my sleep.

* * * * * *

Not long after that weekend, my parents contacted me. They had received several letters in the mail from newspapers denying me *Combat Reporter* status, and my passport had arrived from the State Department.

"What's going on?" my Dad asked.

I told him I wanted to be a combat war reporter, but later that same day, I received notice that I was officially flunked out of college, so I went home immediately to face the concern and embarrassment from my parents, and waited for my draft notice.

It came in late March 1967. *So, I'm going to be a soldier*, I thought. Hmmm.

I got all kinds of advice from my Dad and his WWII friends. Dad had been a gunnery officer in the Navy on a Minesweeper in the Atlantic. He'd only ever told me one story from his service, about how once when his captain thought it was time to test a depth charge, they all had fresh fish for dinner.

One of Dad's friends suggested that if I enlisted, I could pick my job, rather than just being an infantryman. On one thing they all agreed: never volunteer for anything, especially in Boot Camp.

"Picking my job" sounded interesting, so I went and interviewed each services Recruiter (Navy, Air Force, Coast Guard, Marines and Army). Though I really liked the Navy nuclear program, the enrollment was for six years minimum. That was too long. The Marine recruiter was cool, but his eyes were too close together and decided I couldn't take orders from someone who looked like that. I decided that being a medic in the Army would work.

The Recruiter told me that after medics school, I could apply for their dental program, and spend my days at the Army dental clinic at Fitzsimons Army Hospital in Colorado, and go skiing every weekend. This sounded like a plan. So, I enlisted for three years in the U.S. Army as a medic with brand-new plans to become a dental technician and skier.

Back then, not many drafted people were going to Vietnam. Experienced units went and new recruits replaced those units from Germany and Korea, among others, at that time.

Later someone told me, "If you wanna make God laugh, tell Him your plans."

3   FORT BRAGG

AFTER MY PHYSICAL, I GOT MY ORDERS TO take a train from the Philadelphia station to Fort Bragg, North Carolina. I had never been to North Carolina and it sounded interesting. We all got on the train wearing our civvies and with a small bag of toiletries and one change of underwear. The train arrived in Fayetteville where Army personnel escorted us to their busses. A short while later we arrived at Fort Bragg. When our bus stopped, I looked outside and saw what I thought were state troopers. They wore army clothes but with greenish large brimmed hats.

After the bus door opened one of them stepped in and yelled that we had fifteen seconds to get out! Some of us threw bags out the window as we rushed to get outside. Other troopers stood nearby, yelling, "Get in line! Stand at attention!" We glanced at each other and then stood erect. The trooper on the bus introduced himself as Drill Instructor Mathis. I remember distinctly how he said, "There are two things in this world I can't stand: flies and mosquitoes. But compared to new recruits . . . I LIKE flies and mosquitoes!" He said that leaning over eyeball-to-eyeball with one of us.

From there we were hustled from line to line, getting our duffel bag, our clothes, boots, belt buckle, and finally, the haircut. Four barbers, shaved each of our heads with an electric trimmer in about one minute, then yelling, "Next!"

During the next two days we were issued M-14 rifles and a copy of the Code of Military Justice and the eleven General Orders. We were expected to memorize the General Orders and be able to repeat them at any time when asked by any Drill Instructor (DI). Any time we did something one of the DIs didn't like he said, "Give me ten," meaning he wanted ten push-ups. We did a lot of extra push-ups in the first two weeks. I was pretty fit to begin with, but they worked us.

We learned about "policing" an area, where everyone gets in a line, elbow to elbow and walks over the lawn looking for cigarette butts and other trash. We learned how to polish our brass, make our bed "high and tight," and to never, ever walk on the linoleum barracks floor without first stepping onto cut squares of woolen blankets to skate our way across the floor and back. "I want this floor spit shined every time I walk into this place!" We learned not to wear our "cover" (hats) indoors, and we learned *exactly* how our clothing would be folded and where it would be placed in our footlockers. One DI said, "You think that's your footlocker? It says 'U.S. Army' on it. It belongs to me, not you. And I'll inspect it whenever I decide! You got that, trooper?!"

I made the mistake of saying "Yes, sir!" once and he lit into me.

"First, I'm a sergeant. I work for living. Never call me 'sir'. Second, give me ten!" The only acceptable reply was "Yes, drill sergeant!" They always expected us to be *STRAC*, an Army term for a well-organized, well turned-out soldier with pressed uniform, polished brass and shined boots. Informally, it meant, in Army terms, you were "Uptight." After the war *uptight* became a term of derision used by hippies to describe anyone who was anal- retentive. But for us it was a daily goal.

The physical training (PT) was intense. They taught us hand-to-hand combat, bayonet training, and one-on-one pugil stick fighting. We worked the obstacle course. We learned how to throw a live hand grenade (once) and were forced to march and run with full pack, carrying 70 pounds and a rifle.

The hardest part of Basic Training was the monkey bars—steel bars, with 70 handles going from one end to the other. Beneath the bars was a mud puddle, filled daily with water by one of the DIs. Our task was to complete the monkey bars without getting our boots muddy before every meal. If we dropped and got muddy, we had to go back to our barracks, clean our boots, and perhaps also change into fresh fatigues, before returning to eat. The problem was we only had one hour for the meal. All that cleaning ate into our mealtime, making it tough to finish the meal before it was time to do the next thing. After three days of all but one of us failing; we found that our palms, right where the fingers meet, were blistered and for some, the blisters were popped or the dead skin now gone. We discovered that if we bandaged the gauze covering the wounds with enough tape, it didn't hurt too much. Within ten days we were all making the monkey bars without getting muddy, and that was the only bright spot in the entire training.

Within two weeks we all had a nice crop of new calluses where our blisters had been.

The DIs invoked a code of strict discipline to get us to accept "following orders." Anything was an opportunity to help convert us from civilians to soldiers. They woke us up every morning at 3:30 ("zero-dark thirty") and gave us just thirty minutes to shit, shower, shave, get dressed, make our bed, and form up outside. Every day before breakfast at 6 AM, they checked to ensure all 32 in our company (and 20 companies all together) were accounted for. We were to quickly form lines and "police the area," which consisted of walking across the lawns to search for cigarette butts. If any were discovered, we were to "field strip" the cigarette butt, namely, rip the remaining white paper off the finished butt, pour out the tobacco, and then twist the white paper into the filter (if there was one) and put it in your pocket. DIs hated butts on the ground. Anyone caught dropping a cigarette butt, so we were told, was ordered to crawl under the barracks (which were built up high, on posts), dig a hole three feet deep, and bury it. Once done, the recruit was to report to the DI, who then demanded the butt be dug up to prove it was sufficiently buried. This only happened once in another company of recruits, so we were told.

After hearing that, we all field-stripped our butts.

After a few weeks, the DIs no longer spoke to us like we were trash. We actually had conversations with all but the head DI. He was always aloof. By the fourth week there was general rapport between the trainees and the DIs. In week five of eight, we started answering the DIs with "Yes, sir!" again. They replied with "Gimme ten!" to which we said, "Yes, SIR!" Then we did the twenty pushups that were expected with a smile. This kind of fooling around brought us all closer together.

4   BASIC TRAINING

BASIC TRAINING WAS AN EIGHT-WEEK COURSE. NEAR THE end of it there was the Bivouac: a three-day, live fire exercise. We were all a bit apprehensive about it. There were stories about trainees' accidentally standing up and getting hit by the live machine gun fire. The DIs never denied these stories.

Finally, it was time to do the ten-mile march with full pack and rifle to the Bivouac area. We were mulling around, in a typical "hurry up and wait" routine, when all of a sudden one of the DIs drove up in a two-and-a-half ton truck and said, "I need three guys that can type." Most everyone raised their hands, hoping to avoid the Bivouac. I recalled the advice of one of my father's friends, a veteran of World War II: "Never volunteer in Basic." The DI then picked three of the most obnoxious from our group. We all moaned, knowing those three, of all of us, did not deserve being picked to type while the rest of us did Bivouac. When the three came forward, grinning from ear to ear, the DI said, "You're all on garbage duty for the next three days. We have three *types* of garbage cans!" Then he herded them onto the truck to the cheers of the rest of us.

Bivouac was pretty much as depicted in the movie *Renaissance Man* without the rain. We did all that was asked of us, and it seemed like it wasn't as bad as we imagined it would be.

There was live fire, but it was about seven feet above the ground, so even if you stood up in a panic you still wouldn't get hit. But we saw tracers for the first time. And raw pig guts. And we heard (controlled) explosions. The purpose of the threeday exercise was to expose us to things we would encounter in battle and to prepare us for the visual, smell, and sound effects of war.

Finally we had to finish the Mile Run in full battle gear, including a backpack with bricks, and a rifle for a total carrying weight of 70 pounds. The Army Mess Rule was this: "Take what you want, but eat what you take," meaning, always take enough food but no more. The Mile Run had to be completed in ten minutes. Failure meant repeating Basic Training. Of about 280 of us, only one or two fell out. I completed mine in eight-and-a-half minutes, so I was happy.

The next day we graduated and got our orders.

In the Army, a recruit goes first to Basic Training for eight weeks, where they learn discipline and how to follow orders mostly, but also learn how to do a few things, at least in theory. You also really get in shape.

After Basic Training, each soldier, now promoted to Private First Class (PFC), goes to AIT (Advanced Individual Training). Some go to learn how to drive tanks, others learn how to blow stuff up, some learn how to be an infantryman, others learn how to be a clerk.

My orders were for Fort Sam Houston, in San Antonio, Texas, where I would attend medic school. But before that we all had a week's leave to go home and say goodbye. The only thing I remember when getting home was finding my weight had gone up one pound from just before Basic. I was now at 203 pounds.

Medic school was a ten-week course. The regimen was to get up at 5 AM, make your bed, do the Triple S (shit, shower and shave), get dressed, make sure your brass belt buckle was really polished, check the spit shine on your boots, and check the folds in your fatigues to make sure they were straight. You had to be STRAC. All the while we skated along the linoleum floor in socks, or with bare feet, to keep it shiny with no scuffs. Then you put on your boots and cover to go outside and get in formation. Then the sergeant inspected and took roll call. Each sergeant reports to his commander, who reports to his commander, until the Base Commander learns that everyone is accounted for. We'd then "police" the area, then off for some physical exercise, go eat, and then off to medic classes. There we were taught how to keep someone from dying—not to fix them, but to keep them from dying. It's called "first aid." That was pretty much the daily routine.

On a weekly basis, one of the things we had to do was turn in our dirty laundry and, after the first week, pick up our cleaned and pressed laundry from the DI and stow it neatly in our footlockers. Just like at Basic. While we we're out, some officer would inspect our barracks and each of our footlockers. Socks had to be folded just right, along with everything else. Every footlocker had to look exactly like every other footlocker. And the bed had to be made just right, and high and tight—so tight that if someone dropped a quarter on it, the quarter would bounce, just like in Basic Training.

During the third weekend I dropped off my laundry, but there was no package of clean laundry to pick up. I was without clean laundry for the following week! I told my sergeant, and he said he'd look into it. Then I was off to my routine.

That night I asked the sergeant if he had located my laundry and he said the laundry had no record of it ever arriving! I told him my situation and he said that I had better pass inspection tomorrow regardless. So that night I hand-washed my dirty fatigues and tried to press them without an iron by putting them on the floor and using my hand to try to scrape the wrinkles out of my trousers and shirt. The next day I got in formation and caught hell from my sergeant for rumpled fatigues. However, my belt buckle and boots were polished and shiny. I reminded him of the problem and he said that was my problem, not the Army's. I told him that I was paying the Army for the laundry service (they were deducting it from my pay), so it was the Army's problem, and it was they who were not fulfilling their end of the bargain. I had washed my fatigues and my brass and boots were polished. I had done what was required of me and I had paid them to do their job. I was clean, if not pressed.

"I'm gonna report you to the Captain," he replied. I said, "Go ahead." I was pissed.

While I was eating breakfast the sergeant came in to tell me to report to the Captain's office after Mess. I finished breakfast and went. The orderly in the Captain's office informed me the Captain wasn't there and told me to sit. I sat and waited. And I waited some more.

Eventually, the Captain came in and told me he found me in an unmilitary-like manner and was going to give me an Article 15, a non-judicial punishment provided under the Uniform Code of Military Justice, which I had studied in Basic. With an Article 15 you basically agree you are guilty and accept whatever punishment the officer would apply, ranging from confined to barracks to doing extra drills and runs. I told him I would not agree to that and demanded a court martial. The Captain blanched. I knew that an Article 15 was always below the radar for superior officers, but a court martial would require paperwork sent up higher, placing the Captain on the radar of his superiors. He told me to wait.

I spent the entire day in that chair. It's amazing all the things you can think of if all you can do is sit in a chair. The Captain returned about 4:30 and told me to go to the laundry service tomorrow morning and pick up my laundry. I was then dismissed.

I went back, ate Mess, and then hand-washed my clothes for the next day, just in case. In the morning I dressed. The sergeant rolled his eyes when he inspected me but didn't say anything. After Mess I was dismissed. I told the sergeant the Captain had told me to go to the laundry to pick mine up. He knew and gave me directions to the laundry. It was quite a ways off, and I learned just how big Fort Sam really was.

As I walked I realized that the directions he'd given me had taken me into the female Women's Army Corps (WAC) area. It was really quiet. I came around this one female barracks and standing in the road was a company of WACs at attention getting the once-over from their female sergeant. The only thing I heard was, "Ladies, there's twenty-five miles of cock on this base, and you're not gonna get an inch of it unless we get this drill down!" I quickly moved on, and eventually found the laundry. There, on the counter was my laundry!

After that, I never had any problems with the sergeant, the Captain, or the laundry service again. And I never saw any of the WACs, or they me, either.

5   ORDERS FROM 'NAM

FORT SAM HOUSTON GRADUATED A CLASS OF MEDICS every week. When we first got there, we kept hearing that all the graduating medics got orders for Europe, Africa, even one for the Arctic. None were going to Vietnam.

It wasn't until week eight that any graduating medics were sent to 'Nam. First, ten percent were now going to 'Nam. In week nine, we heard that fifty percent of the medics were going to 'Nam. When our turn came, we all got orders for 'Nam. There would be no dental technician school for me.

We took our orders, then flew standby for home. We had a week. After my week, my Dad drove me to Fort Dix in New Jersey. We shook hands and in I went. The next day we were assembled at the airport and told it was almost boarding time. An hour passed. Nothing. Another hour. Finally a sergeant came out and asked if there were any medics present. I knew not to volunteer so I said nothing. He left, then, came back fifteen minutes later and asked again if there were any medics. I raised my hand. He ushered me into another room. There on the table were all kinds of boxes of needles and syringes, alcohol, and vials of vaccines. He told me it was my job to vaccinate everyone for Tetanus and Diphtheria. I knew this shot was an intermuscular (IM) shot, usually to the arm. But I had never given a real needle to anyone, although I had done a pretty good job filling an orange with saline at Fort Sam once. Now I had a whole plane-full of people to give this shot to, including myself. I never said a word but, within an hour I was an expert at giving IM shots. I did mine to my thigh.

We took off and I looked out the window all the way to Anchorage. The Canadian Rockies were really cool to see. The sun was low and the shadows were long. We landed at dusk. When we disembarked for refueling, I was surprised to discover it was 3:30 PM, and it was dark! Wow. About forty-five minutes later, we re-boarded and took off again.

I grabbed another window seat and looked out as we took off. In the distance I could see all these fires down in the snow. And there were vehicles with their lights on, moving. I realized I was witnessing ice fishing from 1,500 feet. It soon got dark and I fell asleep for most of the fourteen-and-a-half-hour flight.

When I woke up all I could see from my window was the ocean. And clouds. Eventually we passed a large, long, and tall island covered with trees, or at least green. Later I surmised it may have been Formosa.

As we made our landing at Ton Son Nhut airbase, near Saigon, I half-expected to see explosions out my window. There were none. In fact, the place, besides being completely military, seemed normal. There were no civilians except for Vietnamese workers. As I got off, the heat blasted my face. I looked around and saw people going about doing what they were supposed to be doing. No hurrying, no ducking, just moving normally. I was now in Vietnam. A war zone.

After deplaning I discovered some of the passengers were soldiers returning to Vietnam after taking a leave in the USA. They knew where they were going and how to get there, but we newbies were evidently not worth talking to. I didn't have a clue. Someone mentioned the "reassignment area," so we asked around and found our way. We presented our orders to a very overwhelmed E-6 (staff sergeant), who looked at them, breathed heavily and laid them on top of a pile. He told us to go get a bunk and wait. About eight hours later we got our orders.

I was assigned to be a medic at the 36th Evacuation Hospital in a place called Vung Tau. I had no idea what an Evacuation Hospital was, or where Vung Tau was. I was apprehensive but followed the lines and went where I was told. Six of us hopped in a two-and-a-half-ton truck and it headed down the road. We ended up in a convoy bound for Vung Tau where we'd be issued our weapons. I had no idea where it was but considered that it might be in the middle of the jungle.

I took a seat at the rear so I could see outside. The land was flat. It looked tropical. Later, I saw rivers and islands, and boats, some with machineguns mounted on them. Much later I could see dunes. Lots of dunes—miles and miles of dunes. On the other side, I spotted a Navy shipyard with a Landing Ship Tank (LST). These were the same kind of boats used on D-Day to drop off troops and tanks on the beach. I later found out this was a "brown water" naval yard, which housed fast boats for river patrol in the Mekong Delta rivers. I knew then we were near water, deep water. My interest rose.

Finally the dunes ended, and we entered a populated area. Funny-looking threewheeled motorcycle pickup trucks were zooming everywhere. I later learned they were called Vespas. We eventually arrived at the camp, and then the hospital. Six of us got out, and the truck drove off. We looked at each other, then, went in to report for duty.

44th Medical Brigade Shoulder patch   36th Evacuation Hospital (SMBL) patch

6   SEPTEMBER 1967

WHEN I ARRIVED, I FOUND OUT THAT I was an "FNG." A fucking new guy. There was no respect for FNGs. Everyone who saw us KNEW they had less time to do incountry than FNGs. All Army personnel went to Nam for twelve months and as soon as you arrived, you started your countdown to the day you could leave. It was a discreet, and exact number, and everyone knew theirs. Those with larger numbers were FNGs and by definition, you were better than them if your number was lower. The Short Timers (those with less than 100 days left In Country) especially, loved harassing FNGs.

Many Short Timers carried a stick often carved in the shape of a dragon, usually painted black. You could buy them downtown for about twenty cents. At their locker, Short Timers had elaborate calendars marking the countdown to DEROS (Date Eligible for Return from Overseas). They were usually a paint-by the-numbers formatted image where each part was numbered and was filled in on a specific date. When the image was complete it was time to go home. Everyone had a number. Every single day some Short Timer, would come up to us FNG's and say, "I'm a 43, what are you!?" Mine was 362, because that's how many days I had left In Country before I could go back to the real world. There was no respect from Short Timers.

When we arrived, the hospital didn't know what to do with us, things were disorganized. However, I would soon see that it was a great hospital, able to keep wounded soldiers from dying and get them stabilized. Most recovered there and went back to their units. Others, like severe burn patients, amputees, and those with chronic diseases went to Japan or the States for follow- up care.

They assigned us to the sidewalk-building brigade. Actually, we were now eight, six FNGs plus two Short Timers. Building sidewalks made sense, even though it was a *semi-mobile* hospital (i.e., ready to leave in 24 hours, although it had existed in this location for 23 months). At this stage of the build-up in 1967—about 100,000 short of the maximum reached in 1968—if any new locales needed a hospital, the Army would install another one; not move the existing ones around. And sidewalks made moving wheelchair patients easier. So we built sidewalks from 8 AM to 5 PM, with a lunch break. We spent hours digging where the concrete would go, then placing boards where the edges would be, then pounded in wooden spikes and nailed the boards to the spike.

We now had a mold in which to pour the concrete. Our concrete mixer made a lot of concrete, so we always wanted more molding than concrete. We had already driven in the spikes when we then positioned the last two boards to be nailed to them. Our NCOIC (Non-Commissioned Officer in Charge) saw that one board was short by about three inches. I thought we would pull the spike and reset them to fit the board's length. That's when I heard the NCOIC say to one of us FNGs "Look, go down to maintenance and get a board stretcher." The FNG looked at the NCOIC, who was now lighting a cigarette. He looked up at the FNG and waved him on. "Go on!" The NCOIC told me to go with him since my friend would need help carrying it. Off we went. We got to Maintenance and asked for the board stretcher. He looked at us and without blinking said, "Captain Thomas borrowed it this morning. I'm sure he's done with it, so go ask him for it." He gave us instructions on where to find Capt. Thomas and off we went. We followed his instructions: we walked to Ward 4, took the side sidewalk between Ward 4 and Ward 3 and went to the back. When we got there the space was empty. We decided to go into Ward 3 and ask where Captain Thomas was. In we went.

We asked an Army Nurse. She said, "Not Captain Thomas again!" She looked at the orderly on duty and asked, "How many times is that?"

He smiled and said, "At least five times in the past two months." The nurse then explained that Captain Thomas left the 36th over a year ago. She then added that we had been sent on a fool's errand and wanted to know what we were supposed to get.

We said, "A board stretcher."

She laughed, wow what a winning smile she had! Then she asked, "Tell me, exactly how do you 'stretch' a board?" It took both of us about a half-second to realize how dumb we were. We left red-faced but laughing. We were FNGs.

When we got back, the NCOIC and his pal just howled. Oh, they laughed! There was nothing to do but suck it up. There was no sense doing today what we could do tomorrow, and we were running out of places to put sidewalks. We were in no hurry. FNGs.

A week later I was assigned to "A&D," which I found out was Admissions and Dispositions. We were responsible for recording the names of the patients who came in, bagging their clothes and personal effects, storing them, and returning them when they were discharged. I was one of the people responsible for bagging the items, storing them in the bins, and recording it all.

Every morning, I would pick up a list of all the patients to be discharged that day.

Unfortunately, a fair number of patients were never *discharged*. All dead Americans (KIA or Killed in Action) were simply handed over to the Army's GRS (Graves Registration Service). It was the same for our supporting allies. We were never told when any patients died, whether civilian, soldiers, or irregulars (Cambodians or Montagnards working with the Special Forces, or ARVN: Army of Vietnam). So the A&D storage area was getting pretty full by the time I arrived. I have no idea why someone responsible never visited us. I suppose they didn't know we were there. After all, we were in the back, out of view from the A&D front office. Our problem was that the bins were filling up.

We were right next to the helipad Landing Zone (LZ) and the ER (Emergency Room).

One of our duties was to push out the wheeled carts to the LZ, load the litters from the helicopters (Dustoffs) onto the carts, give the Dustoff crew replacement litters, then wheel the patients to the ER. All the while the ER medics were getting details

Offloading a patient at the 36th Evac in 1967

from the Dustoff medic, examining the patients, applying pressure if needed, and sizing up the situations for the physicians inside the ER. Occasionally, a physician would come out and size up a really critical case before he was even off-loaded. The A&D medics didn't touch the patients, unless requested by an ER medic. Chain-of-command, and all that. I was very observant of the treatments each patient was given, and learned about the kinds of injuries that way. Burns and full-body blasts were the most graphic, and this was the first time I'd seen any war injuries in person.

We'd follow the patients in, bag their clothes and personal effects as they were removed, get their name and Serial Number from their dog tags, if they had them. Civilians and irregulars were more difficult to tag, as no one spoke their language to get their name, if they were conscious. All bags were then placed in our bins.

If there were no patients coming in it got pretty boring for a few hours. I was able to read *The Source* by Michener in two weeks and Exodus in one. Getting more bored, I started walking around the A&D and ER areas, just checking things out. Most of the wards, which held about 40 patients each, had either sandbags piled up 4 feet along the perimeter of the outside, or had 55- gallon drums filled with sand. Their purpose was to absorb shrapnel from any enemy rockets or mortars that may be launched.

In front of the A&D area we had, instead, a nice stone wall extended out about 4 feet from the wall. The area was filled with dirt but just weeds were growing. I always thought that a stone wall would just be more shrapnel if a rocket came in, but it was accepted.

I had a green thumb so I took it upon myself to convert the top into a garden. In downtown Vung Tau I discovered a Lady Finger banana cutting. I brought it back and planted it. I watered it every day, and was amazed when a bit later it flowered! The plant only grew about 5 feet tall.

In a couple of weeks bananas started forming, then one day one of them was ripe. It was small, very small, but ripe. That day we had an unexpected inspection from the Executive Officer. As he approached the front he saw the ripe banana and stopped and took it! I was pissed, but said nothing. The next day another one ripened and I had my first home-grown banana. It was the sweetest banana I ever ate. Of the ten bananas that were produced in that bunch, I ate three.

7   A CALL HOME AND A DOWNPOUR

BETWEEN THE ER, A&D, AND THE HELIPAD, THERE was a small building screened on three sides. I never knew what this building was for. I supposed it was a place VIPs could wait for a chopper and not get dust blown in their eyes when it landed. After all, the single wall was on the helipad side. I recall this building because there were two things that happened to me there.

One day all hospital staff, including yours truly, were informed that the Red Cross was going to set up in that building a short wave telephone line to the States for one day. The radio operator connected to a network of worldspanning ham operators, with the final ham operator in the States. He would take your number, dial it, and if anyone answered he'd hook it up to the radio and you could have a telephone conversation. You were allowed a five-minute conversation. The only rule of radio communication was to say "Over" when you were done with your part of the back and forth, since it was one-way at the time.

My time came and I called home after being in Nam for about three-and-a-half months.

My Mom answered and we talked. There was a lot of clumsiness with the "Over" part but we got through it fine. I have no recollection of what the conversation was about, other than "I am fine, don't worry about me," kind of stuff. It was great to hear my mom's voice. I'm grateful to the Red Cross for setting that up.

The second time, I was out at the helipad, just checking out the grounds since there was nothing else to do. On one side of the helipad was a ditch. It mostly drained gray water and runoff from the hospital grounds. It was usually just puddled with pools of water, unless it had just rained, which was often. To the right of that was the approach direction for the Dustoffs.

This was barren flat ground, perfect for a chopper approach. To the right of that was another unit, or at least part of a new unit, being set up. Then, there was A&D, ER, the screen room and my garden, which was always being blown by the winds generated from the rotor blades of the choppers. Not all the choppers bringing in wounded were Dustoffs; many were the Huey gunships used to carry troops to and from the field. All the Dustoffs were unarmed and marked with a red cross on the nose and the side doors.

As I scanned the area, I looked up and saw a cloud, a perfect puff of cotton in the air. I love clouds. It was billowing upwards, but slowly so that you would only notice that if you watched it closely, which I did. Within a few minutes the cloud had turned dark on the flat underside and the top had started to flatten out as well. I learned later this is called "anvilling" when the top reaches a cold air layer that blocks any further upward motion and the cloud is pushed laterally against the bottom of that layer. By this time, the cloud was overhead, and it began to rain for twenty minutes. I ran to the screen building and got out of what was, by then, a complete downpour. There was no wind, just rain. It soon started coming down even harder. I had never seen it rain so hard. There was so much rain that I could no longer see the A&D building.

A bit later and I couldn't even see the stone wall of the garden, which was only five feet away. Then I couldn't see anything at all. I was curious. I stepped into the rain. I wanted to feel it and be in it. In two seconds I was drenched, but I was happy. I stuck out my hand at arm's length and could not see it. Five minutes later, the storm was over, the cloud had moved on, the sun was shining, and the ditch was nearly filled with brown water. And I was soaked.

8   A SANDBAGGING PARTY AT VUNG TU

IN ADDITION TO SIDEWALKS, THE 36TH NEEDED MORE sandbags. Two new wards were added, a burn ward and a civilian ward. Since rocket attacks were expected—we had two in the eight months I was there—these new wards needed sandbag revetments surrounding them to protect inhabitants from exploding shrapnel.

The Colonel of the hospital ordered a sandbagging party. Three two-and-a-half ton trucks carrying about twenty of us plus ten cases of beer headed for the beach. Twenty of us off-loaded the shovels and empty sandbags and proceeded to fill them. It can actually go pretty quickly if you have a lot of helping hands. In three hours we had filled the trucks, with still enough room for all of us. Unfortunately, the beer was gone.

One of the guys riding in our truck was a real Short-Short-Timer, those who have less than one month left In Country. His typical comment when arguing with someone above his rank was "Watta ya gonna do, send me to 'Nam?" He had about five days to go. He was anxious to get home, fed up with the military, obnoxious, and just didn't give a shit, because he was "short!" and "getting out of this fucking country." He saw a kid riding a scooter. He picked up a sandbag and yelled, "Hey, gook!" The kid turned just as the Short-Timer threw it at him. The kid swerved, avoiding the hit.

"Damn!" yelled the Short-Timer. "Next time I won't warn them." Thankfully he still missed when he threw the next bag. We all looked on in stunned silence. Then he picked up another sandbag and yelled at the top of his lungs, "You won't have me to fuck around with anymore!" This next throw hit a makeshift concession stand, collapsing it. Items for sale scattered across the street.

At that point the driver stopped the truck. He got out, came back, and told the Short- Timer he was on report, which meant he'd get an Article 15. The Short-Timer made a grimace, shook his head, and when the driver turned, gave him the finger. The driver said, "I saw that in the mirror, you asshole!" and gave him the finger back. The Short-Timer turned to the rest of us, smiled almost ashamedly, and said, "Whatta they gonna do, send me to 'Nam?"

The work at the 36th settled in and became routine. I worked every day from 6:00 AM until 6 :00 PM. I got up at 5:00 AM, triple S'd, got dressed, walked to the cafeteria, said hello to the cooks, went to the refrigerator, grabbed a paper quart of reconstituted chocolate milk and a half-pint of reconstituted milk, and drank the chocolate milk on the way to A&D. I tossed the empty container in the trash can when I arrived and walked over to the coffee maker and, if available, poured myself a cup of coffee, leaving the half-pint of whole milk by the coffee pot. I then went back to the rear where the bins and our "office" were, opened my book, and continued reading, unless I noticed that something out in the front garden needed my attention. It was simple; it was routine. It was safe.

In the evening, after work, I would often leave the base alone and hitch a ride on one of the Vespa taxis for downtown Vung Tau. It was amazing, at first. But it got boring really quick. There were bars everywhere and I soon learned that each bar had its own clientele.

My first night I walked into the first bar I saw. There were a lot of Negros there. I went up to the bar, ordered a drink, and the Vietnamese bartender looked at the guy next to me and gave him a questioning look.

The black sergeant said, "Just this one time." Then he looked at me and said, "Alright, cracker, what the fuck are you doing here?"

I had no idea what was up, so I said, "I'm getting a drink. I'm new in town and just checkin' downtown out. What about you?" I asked, earnestly.

He smiled broadly, then turned to everyone else, and in a loud voice said, "Hey, everybody! This fucking cracker wants to know why I am fucking *here!*" Everyone looked at me and laughed. I still didn't know what was going on. I certainly didn't expect *that!* The bartender brought me my drink, a whisky-Coke, and I paid. The sergeant turned to me and said, very sarcastically, "The reason I am fucking here is because fucking crackers like you don't fucking want me any fucking where else!" Then he got angry. "Now, finish up your fucking drink then get the fuck out of here!" Welcome to Vung Tau.

The next bar I visited was filled with Australians. When I walked in, they called me "Yank," and we had some beers together. No problem. I discovered US Air Force bars,

US Army bars, American Negro bars, Aussie bars, ARVN bars, and one Vietnamese Marine bar. There were no Negro Air Force or Army bars, just Negro bars.

When I was growing up, my parents had been involved in resisting segregation. We even had African students from Lincoln University come stay with us during the holidays when the school was closed. In my experience, blacks, or as I called them then, Negros, were cool. It bothered me that blacks were treated, and behaving, differently. I had no clue what to do about it.

* * * * * *

Vung Tau was at the end of a seven-mile peninsula. At the very tip were two extinct volcanoes. I hired a Vespa to take me out to the tip several times, a good half-hour drive each way. I would explore, then, eventually, walk back to town and get a Vespa taxi back to the base. Each time I found something cool—a nice beach, a great rock out crop overlooking the South China Sea, an old, abandoned, French concrete fort now covered in overgrowth, nifty looking black rock crabs, on and on. I eventually found a nice place where I could sit, and when the South China Sea was angry, I'd watch the waves crash upon a small rocky island just seventy- five yards out. It soon became *my place*.

Military structure on Vung Tau beach, 1967

The first time I was there, I realized there was an old, abandoned, man-made military structure built into the tiny island. A little research and some asking around led me to discover that the Japanese, during WWII, and the French afterwards, had been there. I realized that some military had been here, on and off, for quite some time. I started wondering if there had been any previous battles, and if so, had anyone been killed, and if so, who were they? At My Place, I could just let my mind wander. It was great. No worries.

9 AT THE BEACH

I USUALLY MADE A WEEKLY DAY TRIP TO the beach. Since Vung Tau was an incountry R&R location, there were always GIs here for a few days off. They all went to the beach. I soon discovered the times and days the beach was empty and chose to visit the beach then. I liked solitude, and I liked nature when I could have her to myself.

When I was eight years old my parents sent me and my brother Leslie (I called him Les) to the YMCA Camp Tockwogh (pronounced *tock-wah*) on the Chesapeake Bay. Every afternoon we ran down the trail to the shore to swim. It was one of the peak moments of the day. That's where I learned "the buddy system," which had to be used anytime we were in the field.

One day we went down only to find all these jellyfish washed up on the beach. The water was filled with them. Our camp counselor said, "No swimming today." So we just milled around the beach, getting our feet wet and making sand castles. I was walking around and looked at one of these, now hated, jellyfish. It looked like a very large blob of clear snot, just lying on the beach. I proceeded to get myself a stick and start smashing this ruiner of my afternoon. The counselor came by and asked what I was doing. I said I was killing this pest. He said, "No, you're making more of them." He explained that by cutting up a jellyfish, if any parts of it got back into the water, say by the next high tide, then each piece would become a new jellyfish.

Worried that my actions might help ruin tomorrow, I asked the counselor if he had something I could pick it up with and throw it higher up the shore so it wouldn't be washed into the bay with the next tide. He explained that jellyfish can't sting when out of the water, so just pick it up and throw it to higher ground. I took all my strength and girded myself, then reached down and scraped the sand, gathering all the mangled pieces. It didn't sting! I then lifted the double handful of pieces and threw them up on the dry sand, and said, "There!"

Years later I found myself at the 36th. The beach was a common destination. To me it was pristine. On the right it ended before the volcano, and on the left it curved slightly and seemed to go on to the mountains at the horizon. It was a perfect curve. My eye just wanted to follow it. Nearby were some concrete ruins. In one place there was a large iron plate, which covered, I assumed, a pit. On top of the pit was situated a mama-san selling bananas. Twenty or thirty GIs were usually already there when I arrived.

There was this kid carrying what was called an idiot stick, though I have since realized it's a derogatory term. It's actually a yoke, cleverly used by the Vietnamese to carry two heavy buckets or two filled baskets balanced at the end of the yoke and placed on their shoulder. It was a great way to carry a lot of weight. You could also rotate the stick around the back of your neck, moving the load from shoulder to shoulder. Very clever.

Anyway, this kid had two baskets filled with pineapples. He was selling them for ten dong (about 2 cents) apiece, so I bought one. He proceeded to cut the green leaves off its stalk with his machete, then macheted the rind off the fruit. What he gave me was a pared pineapple with a handle! I proceeded to bite into it and instantly realized that this was like no other pineapple I had ever eaten. It was actually ripe. It was soft and juicy and sweet; the juice flowed down my chest, and was oh-so-delicious. As I continued to eat, the juices just rolled down my chin and dropped onto my chest and toes. Who cared?

When I was done it was just a matter of getting into the water and washing it all off of myself. What a joy.

The beach that day was spectacular. No GIs were there. The water, also known as the South China Sea, was as flat as glass. Not a wave, or ripple, in sight. I walked down to the water and just looked at the dead calm water. Then I realized there was no wind either. I put my right toe in the water and gleefully watched as the ripples propagated out to sea. I wondered how far the energy of that wave would go. Then, immensely pleased, I ran into the sea and began to swim. I did this for a while.

One time I came up and there in front of me was a small bluish-pink, oblong orb. I recognized it as a Portuguese-Man-O-War. The bladder was about one-and-ahalf inches long, but I had read the tentacles of these critters could be very long. I backed away from it, and I was so curious. I wanted to see the whole thing and just see if the tentacles were as long as the *National Geographic* magazine said.

I swam back to shore and found a stick about 5 or 6 feet long. I got back in the water with this stick and waded toward the pink "jellyfish." I then swept my stick under the Man-O-War and knew I had snagged the tentacles when the bladder started moving. I made my way back to shore, confident that the tentacles were well behind me. As I came out of the water, I lifted the stick and examined my prize. The bladder hung down about four inches on one side of the stick, and the tentacles hung down all the way to the water at my feet and coiled some.

I recalled what my counselor said at Tockwogh about "Jellyfish can't sting you out of water." So I walked up to the dry sand and turned to walk down the beach, all the while admiring my catch perched at the end of my stick, held high. Just then, a strong gust of wind came up and blew the tentacles, which were dangling in front of me, across my belly. Before I knew what happened, I was doubled over in a ball lying on the beach holding my stomach with tentacles still stick to me. I could not believe the intensity of the pain!

Once I got my bearings I took the stick and scraped the tentacles off my abdomen. By this time, a welt stretched across me from one side to the other; this enormous welt was about an inch wide and was raised close to half an inch above the rest of my skin. The entire area was a deep red-purple. I washed my stomach in seawater (which turns out to be the right thing to do). Once composed, I went over to the Man-O-War. I picked it up with my stick, went up to dry sand, dug a hole, and buried it.

It wasn't until later that I learned that Man-O-Wars are not true jellyfish; it's a siphonophore, and with them, the rules of jellyfish do not apply. I have still not been stung by a jellyfish out of the water, but my life lesson was this: Don't generalize when you don't know for sure.

10 BEACH DISCOVERY

ONE OTHER TIME I WAS AT THE BEACH at Vung Tau I was kinda bored. I built a drip-sand castle. The sand didn't work like the sand at the beach at Fenwick Island, in Delaware, where I learned to build drip-sand castles in 1953. I could get the plops of sand much smaller here, and the arches I built were very lacy and, in my mind, exquisite. But being so lacy, they dried out quickly and collapsed.

I was still bored. I looked down the beach and saw it just curving off to nowhere. I decided to walk in that direction. I walked for quite a while and the beach didn't change much. When I looked back I could see that I was now, actually, in the curve I had seen a while back. I went on. A while later I could see that there was a big rock just off the beach in the sea. My interest grew as I approached it and realized it was not a rock, but a very old, very rusted, tank. It looked like an old M24 light tank made by the USA and lent to the French. The short barrel was pointing down and toward the beach, like it had done its last stand there.

I also noticed stones here and there on the beach. I approached the nearest one and saw that it was the rusted tail end on an unexploded mortar. I confirmed that the other three were as well. They were angled with the tail end leaning towards the dunes behind. I surmised that the mortars had been fired from the dunes towards the tank. I guessed that this was the remains of some long forgotten battle of the French Indochina war of the '50s in which real people fought and died. I considered looking inside the tank to see if there was a skeleton, but decided against it. I knew that unexploded ordinance, no matter how old, could still explode and I didn't know where it all was. I recalled hearing about unexploded bombs still being dug up in London.

I walked towards the dunes. I wanted to get a full view of the battle scene. Halfway up the dune I heard someone shouting in Vietnamese. Remembering my John Wayne movies, I took off my cover and crept to the top of the dune and peeked over. There was a group of some kind of Vietnamese soldiers, with guns, facing perpendicular to me. Someone else was facing them and talking quickly.

I had no idea who they were. Their uniforms were none that I recognized from all the Vietnamese troops I had seen in Vung Tau. I immediately concluded they were Viet Cong preparing to attack Vung Tau! I gingerly climbed down the dune, knowing they could have seen me and shot me, and started trotting back the way I had come. I told a couple of people I worked with what I had seen and they said, "Don't worry about it. Nobody attacks Vung Tau!" That night I discovered they were exactly right, although we had been rocketed a few months earlier.

11 MEMORIES DOWN THE DRAIN

I BEGAN TO GET A SENSE OF WHAT to expect at the hospital. In addition to receiving combat- wounded personnel, every night the ER would treat at least one gunshot or stab wound after a fight in one of the downtown bars. The rest of the time patients arrived from battles by Dustoff choppers a few at a time, with several hours between flights. Sometimes we got Army GIs, sometimes brown water Navy and Coast Guard, sometimes Australians, sometimes ARVN (Army of Vietnam), and sometimes Koreans. Once we even got a Filipino and an Air Force pilot. As a medic with the A&D, I wasn't actively involved in treating casualties.

Then one day the radio barked and we were told to expect a lot of casualties. The word went out, everyone got into their position, and we waited. When the Dustoff came in, we rushed out, off-loaded the patients, and got them to the ER. After that Dustoff left another landed. Then another. And then another. The doctors called for more hands to replace us medics in A&D so we could assist with triage. The first goal of triage is to identify those near death and keep them from dying. One physician and two nurses came outside and started telling us where to put patient litters. The doctor told us, "Put the head wounds back there, unless they're bleeders. They are NOT an emergency! Bleeders here," he pointed. "All other trauma here! Put the ambulatory ones in the screen shed. Now let's get to work, people! We need to work this problem!" It was clear that they'd deal with head wounds later. The task at hand was to keep all the incoming patients alive and then to get them stable.

We hadn't ever seen anything like this before. I learned later that this was the start of the Tet Offensive of 1968, one of the largest military campaigns of the Vietnam War. Though we couldn't know it at the time, there were multiple battles going on across South Vietnam. But there was no time to wonder. We offloaded patients all day. We probably had a hundred patients in the triage area outside the ER at any one time.

One fellow came in with a head wound so we took him to the back area where the head wounds went. Later, when things had calmed down a bit, and the backlog, except for the ambulatories, had been seen and treated, I recall seeing a physician going through the head wound patients. He called for litters, directing as to which ones needed care next. "Him, him, and this one. Take them inside." Once they got through those and sent them off to Pre-Op, the doctor selected other head wound patients for movement into the ER. Eventually, we were left with just one. The doc asked me to take his pulse and when I did there was none. "Damn," said the doc and he walked back into the ER. I looked at the dead GI. His skull was open and his brains were exposed.

We were told more might be coming, so I had to clean up the area. I started hosing down the triage area, and it took a long while to get all the blood washed into the drain. I moved the dead GI's litter by dragging it so I could wash the area where he had been. When I did, part of his brain slipped off the litter and onto the cement.

They came to haul him away to ER to prepare him for Graves and Registration. The area where his litter had been was bloodied again, and I continued to hose the area once they hauled him away. There was also that little piece of brain there too, about the size of a small chicken nugget. I hosed everything over to the drain.

I finally got all the blood washed away. But there was still that piece of brain stuck in the drain catcher. I squirted it really hard, but the water pressure wasn't all that great. After hemming and hawing, I finally went over, and with my boot, gently pushed the brain piece down through the drain catcher. As I did so, my mind rushed with images of his memories, so neatly stored in this part of his brain being completely destroyed as I pushed with my boot. His Mom, Dad, birthday parties, who knew what memories were in there? In my own mind, I wondered.

I thought a prayer without any words ever forming in my mind. Then I turned and went on to see what else I had to do. As I walked, I saw the ditch by the Dustoff LZ. It was crimson red with American blood. It flowed slowly toward the sea. I felt sad, but there was nothing I could do. I moved on. "More casualties on the way," I heard someone say.

12 CIVILIAN PATIENT

LATER, NEW PATIENTS ARRIVED FROM THE ONGOING BATTLES and from some new battles.

Relating them all would constitute, for me, "war porn" and so I won't. But one patient came in whose story is worth repeating.

When we reformed the triage area with the new influx of patients, we also had a lot of civilian casualties. I had already learned that in Vietnam not just the patient goes to the hospital, but at least one family member too. In the Vietnamese hospitals there were no cooks, and no one to bring food to the patients. The family members had to go get the food and feed it to their patient.

One of the Dustoff medics told me that when onloading a civilian into a Dustoff, you had to make room for a family member. Otherwise, the family would crowd around the chopper and demand either one of them goes or the patient come off. He complained that he could only carry half as many civilian patients in a chopper load because of the extra family members. It made for more trips and longer times for some patients making it to the hospital. So in the triage area we had a de facto civilian area with half of them unharmed but taking up space and getting in the way. We just lived with it.

I saw one very old, very thin man holding a child in his arms. He was still and quiet, just holding the child. I went to take a look for sorting purposes and the child's face was covered. He looked to be young, around five years old. I pulled back the cover and saw that a bullet had plowed a path across his face from his chin to his brow, going right through his front teeth and nose. His eyes were not damaged. I thought he was bleeding pretty well from a lot of places and the standard pressure application wouldn't suffice. I brought this boy's condition to the attention of a physician. He examined him and said, "Right, inside." I had made a good call. I took him in and they dealt with the child right away, ahead of some of the soldiers.

A couple of weeks later I asked about the child and they told me he was stable. Since I was assumed to "like" the Vietnamese they asked me to help in the child's physical therapy. It turned out my job was to teach this boy to play ping pong. The grandfather was with the boy always. I learned the child's name was "Win," which I later learned was spelled Nguyen. From then on, I took one hour off from my A&D work and taught Nguyen how to hold the paddle, and how to hit the ball. He was a quick study.

By the time I left the 36th, Nguyen was able to return the ball to me over the net repeatedly. I have a Polaroid picture somewhere of him hugging me. I hope I find it. Years later I met one of the nurses from that time online and she told me that Nguyen had had several plastic surgeries and his nose and teeth had been replaced. His injury occurred in 1968 and we left 'Nam in 1975, so he had had seven years of follow up plastic surgery. One small victory . . . for a while.

The ER can be a pretty boring place when there are no incoming patients. One of the ER physicians was an older man and I was showing him the small garden I had planted in front of the A&D office. He asked me if I was drafted and I told him that I f lunked out of college and after getting my draft notice I enlisted to be a medic. He smiled, then said he was drafted. I looked at him with some awe and he added, "In fact, I was drafted twice." I didn't understand how that was possible and asked him to explain. He told me that his first draft notice came for the Korean War and he was a basic grunt, an infantryman with a CIB (Combat Infantryman's Badge) and a Purple Heart. After Korea he eventually got his medical degree and in 1966 he was drafted because he was now a physician and the Army needed Docs. So here he was. He was one hell of a good surgeon. The only Doc I ever knew in Vietnam that also had a CIB.

13   LOST AND FOUND WALLET IN VUNG TAU

I HAD BEEN IN VUNG TAU A LITTLE over six months. I went downtown a lot, probably every other night after work. I watched people a lot, and I counted. I'll count anything. One evening I was counting street children—there were over fifty—when I noticed an older kid who seemed to be bossing the other waifs around. I had seen him around before. This time he had an ugly cut on his hand.

I went over to him and tried to explain that I was a medic and I wanted to inspect his hand. He was very suspicious, but let me look. It was a nasty cut, susceptible to infection. I'd been examining his arm for about sixty seconds when he pulled his arm away and ran off. The next day I made sure I had everything I need to fix that cut if I saw him. I actually went looking for him. Hours later I found him. I told him what I wanted to do and he let me. When the wound was bandaged, I told him to find me later so I could check up on him. He looked at me suspiciously, but nodded.

The next day was my day off and I went to the beach. As usual, I undressed, put on my swim trunks and jumped in the sea. Afterward I ate a fresh pineapple, went back in to clean off, then came back to build some of my world-famous (so I imagined) sandcastles. The sun got lower and I decided to change back into my uniform and head back. As I dressed, I realized that my wallet was missing. *Damn!* I thought. Someone stole it! *Fuck.*

The next day I inquired about getting new IDs and went back to work. That evening I grabbed some of my MPCs (Army money), stuffed them in my pocket, and went to town. It was another night in Vung Tau: girls, beer, whisky-cokes, and visiting my favorite Aussie bar.

The next night, I was back in town after a day at work when I saw the boy with the hurt hand. We talked and when I examined his wound, I could see it was on the way to healing. He was quite agreeable this time. Every once in a while some younger kid would run up to him and show him what they had. He'd take one thing and let the kid keep the rest. I learned they were all orphans, and this was how they made their living.

It dawned on me to ask if any of those kids had taken my wallet. I really needed my IDs and Social Security card, plus my photos. He said he'd check. The next day when I saw him, he handed me my wallet. It still had everything inside, including my money, maybe twenty-five dollars or so. I was surprised and really glad. I took all the cash out of the wallet and gave it to him. He looked at me confused. I said, "Sometimes life is good to you. Take it." He did, but he looked embarrassed.

Then he said, "You number one!" It was the best compliment any non-Englishspeaking Vietnamese could give you. I thought, *This kid is decent. All he's trying to do is make a living.* We remained friends until I left.

14 THE ABANDONED PLANE

TET 1968 IN VIETNAM WAS A MESS. General Giap's military offensive against the Republic of Vietnam (RVN) forces and allies was bold. It caught everyone by surprise. But that does not mean it caught us off guard. The ensuing battles created all kinds of messes: broken people, ruined buildings, lost and destroyed equipment. It was a military nightmare for most of us. Then afterwards, it was a paperwork nightmare.

At the Vung Tau airbase there were several airplanes parked on the runway during emergency landings made by wounded flight crews. When they were evacuated the planes were just moved off the runway. After Tet 1968, the planes were returned to their appropriate commands, except one. The Base Commander was told that one of the planes remained, technically, unaccounted for. This C-7 Caribou aircraft was a twin-engine, very useful in the front lines because it was a STOL, meaning "short takeoff and landing" airplane. It didn't need much of a runway, or road, or field to take off. It had a lot of wooden parts.

The one at the end of the Vung Tau airbase runway posed a problem. By the time they had determined the unit it belonged to, that unit said they had already written it off and reclaiming it would be a paperwork mess. So they refused to take it back. That left the Base Commander with an airplane and no one to own it. He told his Sergeant Major to "get rid of it." Later that SGM was in a high-stakes poker game with some Australians and he added the plane to the pot. They agreed. The SGM strategically lost the hand and that Aussie took control of the plane. He painted it white, made it airworthy, and had a civilian Aussie friend fly it off of the base. That took about two months. All to avoid Army paperwork.

15 A CHAT WITH AN ARVN OFFICER, OR WAS HE A VC?

ONCE I WAS WALKING TOWARD DOWNTOWN VUNG TAU when I decided to go down a residential street I had passed many times but never took. At the next block I turned and walked some more, checking out the fence—everyone had a fence around their property—the trees, the plants, and gardens. One yard had very spindly roses growing in the shade. The plants were thin, tall, and leggy. Each one had a growing tip with a small rose bud developing. I looked at it for quite a while.

Then, a young man, maybe three years older than I was came out. He asked me what I was doing. "Admiring the roses," I said. "Oh!" he replied. "You must meet my father, they are his," he said in perfect English with little accent. He opened the gate and let me walk in. We went to the front door and he opened it and gestured that I enter. In I went. We entered a room where a very old, wizened man was sitting on a pillow on the floor. The young man spoke to him in Vietnamese and then the old man began to smile. Then he said something back in reply.

The young man turned, looked at me and said, "He says the roses were a gift to his father by the French general many years ago." I thought quickly and realized that was about twenty years ago, or more. I smiled, and then the old man began to ask questions of me through his son. They were all about growing roses. I knew about growing roses, and I told him what I knew.

There was some clarification about "fertilizer," a word he did not comprehend, and he grinned when I said three fish heads six inches below the roots of each plant would work fine. By that time the mother came in and served us lunch—a pile of fried rice with a partially fried egg on top. I watched the others pierce the partially cooked egg white and let the juices run down into the rice, then they mixed the rice. This was gross to me, but I went ahead and did that too. I didn't die from the experience.

All kinds of conversation back and forth took place. I had grown orchids for a while, and I learned the Vietnamese word for orchid was "wa lan." The son asked me what I liked about Vung Tau. I told him about My Place and he then offered to drive me there on his small cycle.

So we left and went to the ocean. When we finally reached My Place, we took in the view. We sat, and I smoked (he didn't), and we talked for several hours. I learned he studied English and aeronautics at the University of Arizona. He had been on an officer exchange program at the time. He said he was in the Vietnamese Air Force, but on leave.

Eventually, discussion turned to the War. I told him about an NVA (North Vietnamese Army) POW patient I called Winn in the 36th. He was still recovering and needed PT (physical therapy). Since there were no PT personnel to train him, I started playing ping pong with him. After each session we had talked about things and I asked him what he wanted to do in his life. He'd told me in pidgin English that he would "Grow rice." He added that he wanted to have kids, grow a long gray beard and have his grandchildren pull on it.

My new friend smiled at this story. Then he asked, "How do you know I am not VC?" I took a breath. I looked him square in the eye and said, "It doesn't matter; because you and I are not Ho Chi Minh or President LJB. We are people who have eaten together. I have met your family. You and I are friends. There are no politics between us, only gardens."

He smiled, agreed, then said we should head back. I got on the scooter behind him and we headed to town. We came to an intersection where there had just been an accident. A truck had hit a scooter with three people on it. Bodies were sprawled and blood was visible. I told my friend, "Remember I said I was a medic? I'm needed here. Go to town and get someone to send an ambulance!" He left and I went to work. An MP Jeep arrived and we loaded all the injured on and took them to the 36th.

Though I often revisited the rose garden, I never saw my friend again.

16 WHAT I LEARNED FROM THE NGUYENS

BEING A MEDIC IN A HOSPITAL ALLOWED ME to meet people I wouldn't ordinarily meet, and under circumstances that approach a neutrality. I met two Vietnamese men very early in my war experience that summed up the contradictions of this war.

Nguyen Thom (the guy I called Tom) was a South Vietnamese Army (ARVN) draftee soldier who had been at the 36th for nine months when I arrived. He was around my age. His English had gotten pretty good, though he only spoke in phrases and not whole sentences. His unit had been overrun by the North Vietnamese Army (NVA). During the battle, once he was overcome, he was offered an opportunity to pledge his allegiance to the victors of the battle. He refused and was then bayoneted, machine-gunned, and left for dead. On arrival at the hospital, he underwent surgery on his hands, arms, abdomen, and legs.

Once he was allowed out of bed, his physical therapy was to play ping pong. I was one of the medics assigned to play ping pong with him. For weeks we played and soon became good friends. As I'd shared with my rose-growing friend, Tom told me that he hoped to "grow rice" someday and have grandchildren pull on his beard. Tom was sad about the future, though, and quite bitter about how he was treated by the NVA. He was confident that the NVA would lose the war.

The 36th had a separate POW ward where VC (Viet Cong, local rebels) and NVA regulars were kept under guard. At the time, there was only one POW patient: Nguyen Goi. I called him Winn. He was an NVA conscript who was about 19 years old and had been burned by a napalm bomb. After being found he was flown to the 36th, which specialized in burn patients. He was well on the road to recovery, though time would be required to heal him completely.

Winn taught me to play a game called **Cố Thúng**, which translates into Chinese Chess. He was pretty bored. Few people paid any attention to him since he was the enemy. I believe he actually looked forward to our chess matches; of course, he always won.

Like Tom, he too wanted to grow rice and have grandchildren. He told me the NVA had come to his village and drafted him on the spot, without warning. A week later he was on the Ho Chi Minh trail and six months later he was under guard at the 36th. He had no hope of returning and dreaded getting well, for that meant he would be transferred to the South Vietnamese Army and transferred to the Dao Phu Quoc prison where the infamous "tiger cages" were, which we were to hear about later.

We were all drafted into this war, one way or another. All of our leaders were far from the battle, making pronouncements about how evil the other side is, and yet, in the neutral setting of a hospital, all of us were able to get along. None of us had aspirations for power, glory, or domination over the others. We dreamed of growing rice, grapes, flowers . . . and grandchildren pulling on gray beards. Yet the violence they had experienced spoke of something else, something beyond our collective power to avert: we were all victims of somebody else's war.

The only difference I see between Tom, Winn, and myself was that they were drafted on the spot while I was drafted by letter. As every American draftee knows, the "greeting" we received from Uncle Sam was backed up by guns and the threat of jail; and, though seemingly more civilized than just coming into a village and taking away "recruits," the implied violence was just as powerful. Aside from the fact that one always favors their own side in a conflict, the behavior of our three respective governments was the same, and they are equally guilty of the crimes that had been committed against the others.

17 TURNING TWENTY-ONE WITH A BOTTLE OF CROWN

IN MAY OF 1968 I WAS READY TO celebrate my twenty-first birthday. I would finally be old enough to vote! I got a bottle of Crown Royal and planned to go from bar to bar, buying Cokes to pour my own whisky-Cokes. The bars didn't like guys bringing their own liquor, so when they found you doing it, they kicked you out. I figured I could get at least one drink per bar and maybe, if I was lucky, hit all the bars in Vung Tau in one day. That was my plan.

I had the day off, so I got into town about 11 AM. It was early but it was my birthday. I probably should have had some lunch along the way. By 2 PM I was about a quarter of the way into the RC and feeling pretty good. I'd just left a bar and was walking down to the next one.

This next one was a bar for Vietnamese so I would pass it. I happened to look inside through a window out of curiosity and saw, at the far end, a GI lying face down on a couch and being beaten with a bottle by a Vietnamese. I thought, *Whoa, that's not right.* My medic self took over and I walked in right over to the guy doing the hitting, and threw him against the wall. He slid down, knocked out. I went over to the GI and bent over to see if he needed aid. Then I felt someone tapping on my head. I stood up and turned to see a guy standing behind me looking astonished. He was holding a broken beer bottle and pointing it at me.

I knocked him down. The GI was still out cold. Then I saw two Vietnamese Marines sitting at the bar looking at me. Their rifles were leaning against the bar. I thought, *Oh shit, what do I do?* Suddenly in my head I heard a bugle blowing the US Cavalry charge, just like I'd seen in the movies as a kid. I said, out loud, "Right! Go out the back!" Which I did.

When I got out the back door, I was amazed to see that the rear area was all fenced in with no alley between it and the back of the bar on the other street that butted up against this one. Amazingly, all the floor space was covered with upright, empty bottles, packed tight. I tried to walk over them to the fence, which was topped with circular barbed wire. About that time a gunshot went off behind me and the next thing I remember, I was in the back of that other bar as a bunch of Australians were running toward me and the sound of the gunshot, wondering what was happening.

I didn't know it at the time but I was thoroughly bloody. I shouted, "They're killing and maiming on the other side!" Aussies always love a fight and every one of them ran out the front of their bar, down the street and back down the next street to the bar with the fight. I followed them.

When I arrived, three people were already lying on the ground, so I went into medic- mode. One Aussie had taken a gunshot wound to the throat but wasn't bleeding much, and he could speak. One had been knocked out but was otherwise okay. A third one had been stabbed in the throat by a broken bottle.

The MPs arrived. We could only get two wounded in one jeep so the last Aussie was loaded onto a second jeep and then I started to walk away. The MP asked me where I was going. I said, "To my birthday party."

"No you're not," he said. "You're injured too. Get on." I was surprised to hear that, but I was in an agreeable manner.

We arrived at ER at the 36th, where I knew everyone. There was no "GI" among the wounded. Apparently the guy I'd seen through the window was the Aussie who had been stabbed in the throat. He took a while to heal but lived. The knockedout Aussie stayed overnight and was released the next day. The Aussie who had been shot in the throat was released that afternoon. The Doc told me that it was amazing; the bullet had passed all the way through his neck but missed everything that was important. They cleaned and sewed him up on the outside and the inside and noticed that the only thing missing were his tonsils. The bullet had knocked them out. His CO came and picked him up.

Then the Doc said, "Now, let me look at you." I took off my jacket and t-shirt and he said I had a lot of stab wounds on my back. My shirt certainly had a lot of holes in it. When he cleaned out some glass from my back, we decided the weapon must have been that broken bottle. "Now," he said. "Let me take a look at your head."

What? My head? He found seven large abraded lumps, but only one with cuts. "That must have been when the bottle he was hitting you with broke," he said. "Then he stabbed you in the back." He paused, then smiled and said, "Happy birthday." He sewed me up, told me to take some aspirin, and come see him tomorrow. I told him

I wanted to go back to town but he denied that. I spent the rest of my birthday at our EM Club, which was empty except for me and the bar maid. I bought a beer but didn't ever finish it. I got tired pretty early and went to bed. The next morning I woke up with an awful headache. Old enough to vote, eh?

18 TRANSFERRING TO A DUSTOFF UNIT

WHILE AT VUNG TAU, I GOT TO SEE a lot of Dustoff deliveries. I really admired those guys. I asked around and found that any medic could qualify as a Dustoff medic if your MOS (Military Occupational Specialty) was coded 91A. Mine was. The way to do that, I was told, was to request a transfer. So I did. I was told that, because I had already been in country six months, a transfer was out of the question. It took a while to train Dustoff medics (OJT) and the Army wanted a return on their investment. I inquired more and found that there was a way. All I had to do was to sign a piece of paper extending my tour in Vietnam by six months on the condition that I was transferred to a Dustoff unit. I had to think long and hard about that one.

Years earlier I had watched a WWII movie called *The Fighting Sullivans* about five brothers who got along swimmingly and all joined the Navy the same day. They fought to stay together, and later, after Basic and AIT they were all stationed on the *USS Juneau*, a light cruiser. Early in the war, at the naval battle of Guadalcanal, *Juneau* was sunk on the night of November 13, 1942, by two torpedoes. There were only ten survivors, and none of the Sullivans made it.

I had heard that since then, the Defense Department had a rule that only one family member could serve in Vietnam at a time, unless they volunteered. (I was completely wrong about this, by the way). So, I recalled my brother, who was serving in the Peace Corps in Borneo, telling me about one Peace Corps trainee that arrived at his post and a week later got a draft notice. Further, this fellow had to leave the Peace Corps and be drafted.

I thought, *if I extend my tour, Les can't be drafted.* Perfect. I knew he was doing good where he was. So, I signed the extension request, the transfer request, and I wrote a letter to my draft board informing them that they could not draft my brother as long as I was in Vietnam, as I had just extended my tour. So there.

I never heard back from the Draft Board, and they never drafted Les either. So, later, after I had extended one more time, I figured my plan worked.

Two months later, I got my order to report to the 4th Platoon of the 45th Medical Company (Air Ambulance). I was going to be a Dustoff medic.

45th Medical Company (Air Ambulance) patch

19 EARLY DAYS OF DUSTOFF

IT WAS JUNE 1968. I QUICKLY LEARNED THAT travelling with orders doesn't mean much when it comes to getting transportation. I ended up going to the Vung Tau air station around 11 AM and asking around. The dispatcher told me there was a flight scheduled for Ton Son Nhut airbase near Saigon, but the flight was full. He pointed to a bench and told me to wait there. He would let me know of any other f lights or passenger cancellations. So I waited. And waited.

I took off my shirt and used it as a blanket with my duffel bag as a pillow. I dozed. Planes would land or take off and I'd wake up, then doze again. About 4 AM a pilot captain woke me up and told me I was out of uniform. I was a deep sleeper back then, and still groggy from waking up.

"Huh?" I asked sleepily.

He said "That's 'huh?' SIR!" I realized I was speaking with a young officer. (New officers are like young colts. They often enjoy—finally—being able to lord over someone just because they can.) I quickly got my shit in a row. Just then the dispatcher came over and told me to hurry, a plane was getting ready to take off. I grabbed everything, saluted the young Captain, and walked hurriedly in the direction the guy pointed.

As I left I heard the Captain and the dispatcher laughing loudly, likely at me. My ride was a chinook helicopter. I got in, they shut the back—at least as much as they could shut the back— taxied, then took off. It was my first time in a helicopter. Unlike the Hueys so well known in Vietnam, the Chinook had two large rotors and was entered from the rear. If Hueys were the flying pickups of the military, then Chinooks were the midsized bus or truck. The continuous squeal of that engine was enough to drive me crazy. It squealed all the way to Saigon.

I made my way to Long Bien and I then found the 45th Company HQ. Later I hitched a ride with one of their Dustoffs headed back up to my destination: the 4th Platoon in Lai Khe, headquarters for the 3rd Brigade of the 1st Infantry Division, the Big Red One, the same division that invaded Omaha Beach on D-Day and took heavy casualties, and earlier had participated in Operation Torch, the invasion of North Africa, and the invasion of Sicily known as Operation Husky. I was in the war now.

Lai Khe base existed in the middle of a rubber plantation. Since the 1st Infantry Division was stationed there, there were about 20,000 of us in all. Our unit had 48 members. During and after Tet 1968, Lai Khe was mortared and rocketed a lot and soon obtained the name "Rocket City." Believe me, there were lots of other places that deserved that name as well (and later I learned they did have that nickname as well). At first, when the evening attacks occurred, we would likely be in our tents, built upon a wooden floor about three feet off the ground. We were building convenient "bolt holes" that led (or would lead, when finished) to underground bunkers. I always jumped into the nearest one and waited when we were being mortared and rocketed.

Often, joints were smoked and that seemed to have a calming effect. Though I don't think I was ever stoned on pot until sometime after I left 'Nam, but it was where I first smoked pot. (Some lab MD ought to look at the effects of pot on adrenaline metabolism).

After a while, I learned to quickly distinguish close and farther away attacks. Our small area of this huge base was not the target of the attacks, so we would often continue what we were doing, ignoring the ongoing attack. But we always took note of where the first mortar or rocket struck. If it wasn't close, then we could ignore it altogether. If it was close, but not too close, then we had to figure out if the second round was closer or farther away. Especially with mortars, for Charlie always mortared in a line. If the second round was farther away, we ignored it, since the line of subsequent rounds would get farther away still. I remember once when an attack came and the mortars were landing about 100 yards away at the hospital. Somebody said, "Looks like it's their turn to take hits," and we continued to listen to the Beatles *Magical Mystery Tour*, our only album, accompanied by the explosions in the background.

20 ROCKET CITY

OUR 45TH MEDICAL COMPANY (AIR AMBULANCE) HAD FOUR platoons, each comprised of six choppers, six medics, six crew chiefs, six ACs (Aircraft Commanders) and six pilots, plus ground support personnel such as the RTO (Radio Telephone Operator), the Platoon commander, usually a major, and his executive officer, usually a Captain or 1st Lieutenant and a few others.

Each chopper belonged to each of the crew chiefs; where one went, so did the other. All other flight personnel were rotated, however, in our platoon the medics were paired with the crew chiefs. We were the 4th Platoon and were originally stationed in Lai Khe. So our call signs would be Dustoff 40, Dustoff 41, Dustoff 43, etc., all the way up to Dustoff 49. Dustoff 46 was always reserved for the Platoon Commander since any call sign ending in "six" was reserved for the commander of that unit. The reason there were more possible call signs than ACs was as one AC rotated out a new AC could pick an unused number, thereby being unique, just like what the university athletes do with their athletic shirt numbers.

The other platoons of the 45th Med. Co. were stationed in Long Bien near Saigon, about sixty miles south of us. From their perspective, Lai Khe was always being hit. From their perspective, going to Lai Khe was like a Russian going to Siberia. From their perspective, Lai Khe was a place to be avoided. This worked to our advantage, since the company Commanding Officer (CO, a Lieutenant Colonel) was in Long Bien. This meant there was less brass around. Our field officers (Lieutenants to Majors) in Lai Khe were focused on the unit performing as it should to complete the mission. Pressed trousers, polished brass, and spit-shined boots didn't help with completing the mission.

With no generals or colonels around, there was no one telling you, "You need a haircut!" No one was pissed at you because your boots were dirty, or that your bed wasn't "high and tight." No one inspected our footlockers; we wore our boots on the floor of our six-man tent.

Inspections were rare. We were in a danger zone, and no one cared if you were STRAC. In fact, people did care if your brass was shiny because Charlie could see the reflections and it would give away our position if we were ever shot down and running on the ground. As long as you were good at your job—and completed the mission—no one cared too much what you looked like. But we did shave every day and made sure our equipment always worked properly. The most important thing was that everyone had to have everyone else's back. That's the only way you can *complete the mission.*

Army Regulations required that all units undergo an annual IG (Inspector General) inspection. This inspection was supposed to assure the higher ups that all was well with the unit, ensuring that our TOE (Table of Operations and Equipment) was accurate. One day, Major Basil Smith, our platoon CO, was informed that an IG inspection was coming soon. We had two weeks to prepare. We busted ass getting ready. When that day arrived we were smooth and clean, STRAC, at least on the surface. The helicopter brought the IG and within fifteen minutes the inspection was over and the IG was on his way back to the "safety" of Saigon. We had passed.

After that, whenever we were in Long Bien on business, we always referred to Lai Khe as "Rocket City" just to reinforce the image and further discourage brass from visiting.

Lai Khe, in the summer, can get pretty hot and humid. One day in late August 1968, we didn't get any Dustoff calls. The weather was hot and humid, and there was no breeze. It had been like that all night too. It was too hot to be in the RTO office so we all were sitting outside in the shade. Finally, one of our ACs, Randy Radigan (Dustoff 41) said, "That's it." He got up and said, "Who wants to go with me?"

"Where?" we asked.

He pointed up. "At 5,000 feet it's a lot cooler," he said. "I need to cool off." All of us not on 1st or 2nd up jumped up and got in the 3rd up chopper. Randy revved the engine and called Lai Khe Tower asking for permission to depart. The tower asked in what direction. Randy said, "Up." Tower said we were cleared for takeoff. And we went up. Straight up.

We soon got to cooler air and started to feel better. We hung around for about 20 minutes at 3,500 feet and started horizontal movement and began our approach to our LZ at Lai Khe. It was nice to get away from the heat, if even for a little while.

This is the only picture I have of Randy Radigan, the best AC ever. WO Randy Radigan, Dustoff 41. (Photo by Tom Cash)

21 SOME DUSTOFF BASICS

AT LAI KHE WE HAD A FIRST UP, Second Up, and a Third Up crew. We also had one chopper stationed at Quan Loi and another at Dau Tieng. All these crews would make field pickups and drop the wounded off at the nearest medical facility—namely any unit where they could be stabilized. Then they would go out and pick up more wounded. If the stabilized patients need to be moved again soon, Third Up would go and get them and take them to where they needed to be, which was usually one of the major hospitals in Saigon or Long Bien.

This was the ideal. But during a big battle creating a mass casualty situation—where 50 or more casualties resulted in a few minutes—all our available Dustoffs would be making field pickups simultaneously. Then, choppers from the 1st, 2nd, or 3rd platoons in Long Bien would be called to make the patient hauls. The Dau Tieng Dustoff chopper would often make drop offs at the 45th Surgical in Tay Ninh or the 25th Medical Battalion at Cu Chi, the Quan Loi unit dropped patients off at the Quan Loi medical facility (I can't recall the unit), and the Lai Khe units dropped them off at the 2nd Surgical in Lai Khe. Patients hauled to Saigon went to the 3rd Field Hospital, or the 24th Evac or 93 Evac. In these cases, we took them to the hospital specified by the physicians at the pickup unit.

The Fourth Platoon had arrived in 'Nam almost a year before as a unit shipped from the US. Now, the entire unit that came over was being rotated back to the States, more or less. So for a while, there was almost double the normal staff in the unit as US replacements, like myself, arrived. One day during this transition period we were out sandbagging when one of the old crew chiefs referred to us as "FNGs." Most of the replacements had just come from the States and they were entitled to that title, but not me. I told the crew chief, "I'm no fucking FNG. I've been fucking in-country for eight fucking months now."

He replied, "So? You're fucking new to Dustoff, so you're a fucking FNG!" He was right. I hated it.

Some of the old crew had extended their tours to remain behind. Just about everyone had a nickname. One AC (Aircraft Commander) was known as Randy "Rotorblades" Radigan (call sign Dustoff 41). They say Randy used the rotor blades to help chop his way down through the trees to get into tight LZs so often that the Army finally sent him a bill for the blades. Of course, he never paid—if, that is, it was ever really sent. Randy never saw an LZ he couldn't land in or hover over to pick up wounded.

Back to the nicknames. Major Basil Smith (Dustoff 46) was "Majo." Captain Owen (Dustoff 43) was "Stretch" because of his height. Lt. Dan Weaver was "Evil Weevil" (Weaver/Weevil. Get it? Neither did I.) Warrant Officer (WO) Stephen Plume (Dustoff 42) was "Feather." WO Marler (Dustoff 47) was "Gramps." WO John Murray (Dustoff 48) was "The Hobbit," then "Dashing," then "The Pruner" for his exploits of chopping trees during hoist missions. WO Gary Mock (Dustoff 49) was "Wonder Boy" because he looked so young. The only nickname among the Enlisted Men (EM) that stuck was SP5 Drexel "Flashlight" Johnson, who earned his moniker after a tussle with some drunken engineers one night who invaded our compound. His flashlight helped win the day that night. We never said the officers' nicknames when they were around.

When we went to pick up wounded, we went to where they were. They were often still under fire and may even be in an area where a Dustoff, or any chopper, cannot land. In those conditions, we used an electric driven hoist to lower a "seat" for the wounded to strap to and we hoisted them up, one at a time as we hovered. We called these "hoist missions." In some cases, we hoisted litters made specifically for that job. Hoist missions in the forests were the most problematic. The unit was probably still engaged with the enemy and didn't have the men or time to clear a landing zone (LZ). They might just blow up one tree trunk and use the created gap to allow the Dustoff to get a little closer to the ground.

The medic was the Chief Medical Officer on board the Dustoff. He was responsible for all medical calls, including picking the appropriate medical destination for the patient(s). In most emergencies it's the closest facility available. The medic's job was to keep the patient from dying; the hospital's job was to repair the wounds and stabilize, then aid in recovery. Crew chiefs and medics were paired off. They always flew together on the crew chief's assigned Huey (UH- 1H Bell helicopter).

pe| LARRY KIPP 63

Dustoffs were essential to the war effort, so they were the first units to get the new 'H' models. Co-pilots and ACs were rotated individually. On any given day, my crew chief and I would fly with any combination of co-pilot and AC on our helicopter. Crew Chiefs also got to name their chopper, because it was their chopper. Where it went, they went. They were mostly named with respect to current social events. We had *Iron Butterfly* to honor the band of the same name, and after it was destroyed, *Iron Butterfly II, Wild Child,* and likewise, *Wild Child II, El Toro, Hover Lover,* and *Flower Power.* Our Dustoff, was never photographed, but was called "The Judge", as in "Here comes the Judge" from Rowen and Martin's Laugh-in.

My crew chief was Tom Cash. He absolutely never wanted to know anything about blood. I remember the day we were paired. We shook hands and Tom asked me if I wanted to see his chopper. "Sure," I said and off we went. At that time his chopper was a new Bell H- model that had not seen service yet. He was pleased to have a brand spankin' new chopper all his own. Tom asked me if I knew about Hueys and I told him about my experiences at the 36th Evac. Hospital unloading patients. He looked at me and said, "So, you don't know anything," and shook his head. We were a team, but neither of us knew it. From then on we stuck together.

Our Hueys had two pilot seats upfront, and two side seats—one on each side in the rear (used for walking wounded) and then open floor space. Medic and crew

Some of our Dustoff choppers. Not shown are El Toro and The Judge. (Photos by Tom Cash)

chiefs sat on "chicken plates" facing backward, back-to-back with the two pilots. The chicken plate protected our butts from bullets coming up from the floor, so long as we were sitting on them.

Tom wanted to completely check out the chopper before we flew in it. That is *completely check out* the chopper. I have no idea how many bolts there are on the engine of a Bell UH-1H engine, but every bolt had brittle torque paint on it to show it hadn't loosened. Using his torque wrench, Tom checked every bolt to be sure it was at the torque it was supposed to be . . . no assumptions. I soon learned that he didn't want me touching anything important to the functioning of his chopper. He gave me one job, "The most important job," according to Tom, of being responsible for keeping the windshield clean at all times.

My main job, as far as Tom was concerned, was to wipe the Plexiglas windshields with a special formula that filled in any nicks or scratches. The first time I had to do that, Tom told me to go to supply and get some windshield washer and, "Oh, get some rotor wash too." I went, got the windshield washer and the Supply Sergeant told me he was out of rotor wash. He said, "But there might be a bucket of it in the RTO (Radio Telephone Office)." I went to our RTO and asked and was laughed out of the place. "Rotor wash" it turned out, is the wind created by the rotating blades. FNG. Damn!

My other task was to clean up all the blood on the floor of the chopper after a mission. I kept a quart of hydrogen peroxide to do the final clean-up on any given day. Sometimes a whole gallon was required. Beyond that, my crew chief wouldn't let me touch a screw, but he did have me help, on a daily basis, to check each screw on my side for torque effects. He had placed torque seal paint on each screw after it was tightened. When it dried it became brittle and if the screw moved, a crack would form on the torque seal. Of course, after he had checked his side (the right side) he came and checked my side. He said it kept him busy.

On our second day together, Tom said that he needed to name his chopper. He threw out a few suggestions and I countered with my own. Because I had some Dutch ancestors I really liked "The Flying Dutchman." Tom did too. At a card game that night in the RTO we offered that to the players. Randy Radigan was playing and he said, "You might spook some people because the *Flying Dutchman* is a ghost ship." Damn, that killed that idea. I cannot remember how we all knew the phrase, "Here comes de Judge" from the Rowan & Martin's *Laugh-In* variety show but we did. In our goofier moments, we would all look at each other and simultaneously blurt

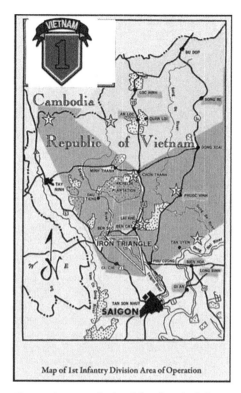

Map of 1st Infantry Division Area of Operation

The area between the last "a" in "Cambodia" and the star with a "2" was called the "Parrots Beak," and the area between Bu Dop and the 1st Infantry Division emblem was called "The Fishhook." The Iron Triangle is depicted just south of Lai Khe. (Image from the 1st Infantry Division)

out, "Sock it to me! Sock it to me! Here comes the Judge!" That happened at the poker game and Tom and I looked at each other and said, "The Judge!" That's when our Dustoff was named *The Judge.*

Our Area of Operations (AO) basically covered all the area where the 1st Infantry Division was deployed. (See the following map, taken from the 1st Infantry Division website.) We had three locations where our six choppers were stationed: Lai Khe (dark blue-green) had four choppers, Quan Loi (light blue) had one chopper, and Dau Tieng (green) had one chopper. The crews at Quan Loi and Dau Tieng flew until their chopper reached the 25-flight-hour limit, then they returned to Lai Khe for inspection and were replaced by another of our choppers. The zones depicted were not hard and fast. If the Quan Loi chopper was doing a mission near Bu Dop and a mission for An Loc came in, Lai Khe may opt to take that mission, since the goal was to get wounded people to the hospital as soon as possible. *Complete the mission.*

22 STANDARD ON-THE-JOB-TRAINING

I STARTED CREWING AS A MEDIC RIGHT AWAY, learning my job as we went along. I remember my first flight. Crew Chief Tom Cash and I hopped on. Tom said, "Clear right." Then everyone looked at me—the AC, the co-pilot, and Tom. Since Tom was on the right, I figured out I was supposed to say, "Clear left." Once the AC heard me and he lifted the helicopter off the ground, having already gained clearance from the tower. We were up!

The first few weeks of being a Dustoff medic were not very demanding. No hot LZs (a landing zone in which we were taking fire), of which we heard countless stories in the RTO shack. None yet. Most of the wounded were shrapnel wounds from mines, road or work accidents, and one stabbing by some irate VC in a civilian village. I am grateful my introduction to being a Dustoff medic was so *orderly*, since I had never, ever, actually diagnosed and treated a patient solely on my own before.

My classes at Fort Sam had been spot on. Clear the airway, stop the bleeding, treat for shock. For heat stroke cases, cool them down rapidly. I learned to have a few bottles of alcohol ready just for heat stroke patients and water to hydrate them. When at the base I made sure everyone I met had taken their salt tablet. If not, I gave them one since dehydration was common. In those first weeks there were no burn patients or amputations. Nor were there any gunshot wounds.

I quickly learned that the only "medical" people in our unit were the medics; everyone else was a pilot, crew chief, radio operator, or supply officer. Of us six medics, the one with the most flight time became the *de facto* "senior medic" and had command over the rest of us. But on our choppers, each of us was *the* medical officer in charge, and was responsible for all medical decisions (such as which hospital to take the patients, based on the nature of their wounds and the need for immediate surgery). No one, not even the Aircraft Commander, could override such a medical decision. I learned all this piecemeal; it was after all, on-the-job training.

One day we flew with Randy Radigan as AC on a mission. We came into a field and picked up a walking wounded. I heard, "Clear right," and I said, "Clear left" and we took off. As soon as we were off the ground, Randy steered the chopper to the left. We almost hit a tree.

Thanks to his flying skills we avoided that tree. He didn't say a word. We dropped off the patient at the hospital LZ, then hovered over to our revetment, landed, and shut down. Randy turned to both of us and said, "I want everyone in the RTO shack, now!"

Randy marched through our compound of hooches and told everyone to meet in the RTO shack. Ten minutes later everyone was standing around in a circle, with Randy at the center. He pointed at me and said, "I won't fly with this man anymore!" I was stunned. He went on to explain how I had cleared the left side of the chopper for take-off, how he went left after lift-off, and almost ran into the tree. Looking at me he said, "It was your job to let me know that tree was there!" Everyone looked at me, silently. Randy then said, "Your flying days are over."

I was still stunned. I realized it was my turn to speak. I had no idea what to say. I simply blurted out, "Wait a minute, nobody taught me anything about crewing! I get here, they say, 'That's your chopper,' and poof, I'm a crewmember. For all I knew 'clear left' simply meant that I was in the chopper and therefore ready to take off! I didn't know it meant anything about trees. How am I supposed to know that?"

It must have been quiet then for at least 30 seconds, but it seemed like an hour. Then Randy blurted out, looking at me, "You're a big dummy!" Then he looked at my crew chief, Tom, and said, "And you're the little dummy!" I thought he was basically referring to our relative body size, I was 203 pounds and Tom was about 155. Then he added, "From now on, nobody flies with the dummies except me!"

Wow. I had just successfully defended myself using argument for the first time in my life. Parents, teachers, principals, and Sunday school teachers . . . they all had a pre-set attitude that would not change during a "discussion." I still didn't think much of myself, but I did quickly learn to respect Randy, who was a year older than I was. My initial embarrassment only lasted about an hour. For the next three weeks, Randy taught us everything he wanted out of his crew members. He was generative about it too.

I realized then that crew training should have been SOP (Standard Operating Procedure). And soon it was. LTC. Arlie Price, our Company CO, issued an official

Memo on 12 November 1968 on the subject: "Responsibilities of Aircraft Crew Members, 45th Medical Company (Air Amb.) And Attachment Detachments" that spelled out the new SOP. It took me almost getting fired and our chopper almost getting trashed in a tree to make that happen. Apparently, Dustoff was still evolving.

For the next while, Tom and I were on First Up anytime the chopper had enough f lying hours before the next 25-Hour Inspection. Randy oversaw everything. He was polite, even friendly after Day 3. Before we took off from the field, he'd look my side over and point out everything outside he wanted to know about before lifting off. I was a quick learner. After ten days, Randy announced that I was fit to crew for any pilot or AC in the unit. He said he'd "bet his life on it." Much later, when I became a Senior Dustoff Medic, I took it upon myself to teach FNG medics how to crew before we let them crew alone. That became SOP.

23 EXPERTISE

ROTORBLADES RANDY ENDED UP BEING THE BEST HUEY pilot I ever knew, and we had a lot of very good ones. Randy once told me that one of the reasons he extended his tour was so he could continue to fly combat missions. Each mission was unique, and most of the flying was by the seat of the pants. He also said that he once read that during WWII the Japanese Imperial Naval Airforce was split into two groups: the old-school upper-class pilots, and the latter, quickly recruited, common citizens. He said the upper-class pilots never talked to the other group. As a result, the newer, common citizen pilots never got any feedback on the lay of the land or quirks and capabilities of the enemies' different plane types. So the newer pilots got shot down quickly because each was relearning what somebody else already knew, but hadn't been taught because of the class distinctions.

He said that every LZ had its own "quirks." He then told me about Hill 1391, east of Thuan Loi, up near Quan Loi. "Never fly west off that hill. You'll get caught in a downdraft and crash right where all the other dead choppers are." He said there were a "gazillion LZs" like that, each unique. Each needing an AC (him) to teach the FNG co-pilots.

Lai Khe Dustoff covered a large area. From Lai Khe, actually a little farther south to the Iron Triangle, we covered 45 miles north to the Cambodian border, including the "Fish Hook" region that was one of the terminals of the Ho Chi Minh Trail, 25 miles west to Tay Ninh City, and 30 miles east to Dong Bo. Also, everything to the west of a line from Dong Bo to Song Be up north to the border. Units we covered were the 1st Infantry Division (aka "The Big Red One" or "1ID"), the 4th Inf. Division (rarely), the 24th Inf. Div., and several armored units, including Black Horse (11th Armored Cavalry Regiment) to our east. One of those units was commanded by the son of General Patton of WWII fame. I actually saw him and the pearl-handled pistols his father used to carry that were now in 'Nam. Later, we also covered the 1st Air Calvary Division, when these units were shifted into our area. Besides Lai Khe, we had two advanced positions where we placed our choppers: Quan Loi to the north, near the Cambodian border and near Bu Dop and Song Be, two scary places to do pickups; and Dau Tieng to the west, halfway to the Black Virgin Mountain, Nui Ba Dinh, Tay Ninh City, and Cu Chi.

24 TEENY WEENIE AIRLINES

LAI KHE HAD TAKEN A REAL BEATING DURING Tet, just a few months before I'd arrived that June. Everyone was still very wary. FNGs learned to be wary from those who were there during Tet. No one who ever told us a war story ever exaggerated, or if they did, we couldn't tell which part was true and which part was not. For FNGs it was better to err on the side of caution, at least for most of us. Major Basil Smith was no exception. He was an FNG and he wanted our compound as rocket-proof as possible. That meant a lot of sand bagging and bunker digging.

Sand bagging is more than just filling bags with sand. You have to borrow a twoand-a- half-ton truck, go to the sand pit the Engineers ran, beg for sand, haul it back. Go to Supply and beg for sand bags. Then we had to dig trenches, line them with boards we had also begged to prevent collapse, cover them over, and then place all the sand bags on top. It was time consuming and labor intensive. Plus we had to fly our missions.

One day a two-and-a-half-ton truck arrived filled with pre-filled sand bags. Cool. The next morning we were told that Third Up was to fly a Colonel down to Saigon. It turned out to be the commander of the Engineers who supplied the sand bags the previous day. A couple of days later a pallet of sawed lumber arrived. Cool again. The next day we had to fly a Lt. Colonel from Lai Khe to Di An. The Lt. Colonel turned out to be the Exec. Officer of the Supply Depot. From then on, our sandbagging tasks were reduced, and our flying of Majors, Lt. Colonels, and Colonels to various destinations increased.

We were done sandbagging, done digging bunkers (bolt holes), and the place was pretty much up to snuff. So we repaired an old building and converted it into our NCO club where we hung around and listened to the only Beatles album we had while drinking warm pop and beer. One day, somehow, an obsolete blood chiller arrived. We repaired it and from then on, we had cold pop and beer. When we had a flight to do for some medical supply sergeant, we decided to call ourselves "TWA," Teeny Weenie Airlines.

25 CARRY LIMITS

WE ONCE GOT A CALL FROM A GROUND unit that discovered a large cache of weapons. They saw us flying by and asked us to help haul out the weapons; otherwise they would have to blow them up.

Our AC got on the horn and said that we were a Dustoff helicopter and could not haul weapons out under the Geneva Convention. They called back and pleaded, "Just this one time."

The AC said, "That's a supply problem, not a medical problem. Over and out."

To many ground troops, we were just another flying pick-up truck. But we were specifically an unarmed air ambulance with a red cross on it. The Geneva Convention states, "(3) The GWS protects from attack any medical vehicle appropriately marked and exclusively employed for the evacuation of the sick and wounded or for the transport of medical personnel and equipment. The GWS prohibits the use of medical vehicles marked with the distinctive emblems for transporting nonmedical troops and equipment."[1] This was one of the rules we flew under.

---

[1] "THE GENEVA CONVENTIONS APPENDIx A," studylib.net, https://studylib.net/doc/10727295/the-geneva-conventions-appendix-a

26 ABOUT AC'S

THE DEPARTMENT OF DEFENSE (DOD) DEFINES AN AIRCRAFT Commander as: "The aircrew member designated by competent authority as being in command of an aircraft and responsible for its safe operation and accomplishment of the assigned mission. Also called AC."

An AC is like the captain of a ship. Nobody can tell him what to do, including those outside of his chain of command, even if they out rank him or her. ACs exist in an aircraft with two or more personnel able to fly the craft. A single seat aircraft is f lown by a pilot. With an AC, the assistant is the pilot. The pilot is usually the FNG. He'll have less seniority, experience, and rank than the AC. Once the mission is over, the crew chief is the boss of the helicopter.

Once deemed ready by the Platoon Commander, a pilot may be asked to take his AC test.

I don't know if there is a written part, but there is a flight part. I've been there. On such a mission, the AC is usually, maybe always, a flight instructor, not just any old AC. He sits where the co-pilot usually sits on the right-hand side. The crew in the back—the medic and the crew chief—are those assigned to that helicopter. The copilot being tested sits in the AC's seat on the left and when instructed, lifts off the chopper and heads to a specified altitude. All the while the Instructor is checking to see if the co-pilot is doing all the things, in the correct order, he should. The medic and crew chief are in the back, facing away from the AC and co-pilot. Our eyes are on what's to the left, right, and rear of the chopper. As well as anything above or below, like another aircraft, or tracer bullets seen coming from the ground, etc.

The sequence is never the same, but at some point, the Instructor turns the chopper engine off when the co-pilot is busy doing something else. The goal now is to make an emergency landing with the engine off. It's called an "auto-rotation."

As the chopper drops, the wind passing the rotor blades increases in speed. If the co-pilot adjusts the blade pitch properly, the chopper will fall faster and the blade rotation will increase. At the same time, the co-pilot has to identify a safe landing zone. Since we are not near the airbase, the landing is uncontrolled and on unknown ground. In theory, there could be mines (IEDs in today's language) or local VC or sappers nearby.

As the chopper falls, the blades increased their rotation, and down speed increases. Just before we touch the ground, the co-pilot is supposed to pull the collective all the way up, thereby changing the blade pitch to gain as much lift as possible (which will always be less than our fall rate since there is no power) to cause the helicopter to almost hover, then gently make contact with the ground. It's kind of like opening a parachute in free fall just before you hit the ground, only different. If the auto rotation is successful, everyone lets out their breath and cheers. If not, the skids might be bent and you'll need to go land on a pile of sand. On the way back, if he passed, the former co-pilot contacts the RTO and declares, "This is Dustoff xx returning to base." In that way, he has declared his Dustoff call sign and announced he's no longer a co-pilot but now an Aircraft Commander. I imagine the official paperwork occurs later.

27 DUSTOFF USUAL PROCEDURES

THE USUAL PROCEDURE WHEN DUSTOFF GOT A CALL for a pickup was for the RTO to get the message, take down all the particulars, then go out and crank the siren to alert First Up they had a mission. The medic and crew chief would go directly to the helicopter and unhook the rotor. As the medic, I'd look over my medical equipment to ensure, once again, that all was right, and Tom would give the bird a once over, looking for leaks, checking the oil level, again, in the tail rotor oil window, etc. By then the co-pilot and AC would have run out, usually with a sheet of paper. They'd call out, "Clear?!" and Tom and I would step out to be seen and yell, "Clear!" and the pilot would then start the engine. Tom and I would push open the engine panels on either side and watch the turbine as it started. Our job was to alert the AC if something was wrong, like fuel leaking and smoking or burning around the engine. Once the rotor was rotating well, we would go to the pilots and slide their side-protecting armor plate (called a "chicken plate") forward and close their door.

Then we would hop in, take one last look around, and then on the headset intercom say, "Clear left" (for me) and "Clear right" (for Tom). This let the AC know three things. a) The engine start-up is okay. b) There are no obstacles to the left or right of the aircraft. c) The rear crew was safely in the helicopter and ready for lift off. During this time the co-pilot was starting the engine while the AC was looking over the details of the pickup. He would radio to ask the tower for permission to take off in "x" direction." The tower would let us know about any other aircraft in our area and then gives us a go ahead and we'd lift off. This whole process took about three minutes.

As the co-pilot flew the aircraft on the permitted flight path, the AC radioed to contact the local artillery control station to ask if there was any outgoing artillery to fly around. They would also give the AC a heads up if we were flying into another artillery zone and about any known activity there, including plane bombing runs and radio frequency contacts. The AC took notes, and if needed, made erasable marks on his map. He then gave the co-pilot more details about our destination, the path to get there, and any details about radio frequencies, etc. Off we went. We usually flew between 1,000 and 2,000 feet elevation—higher when in enemy territory to avoid bullets.

I was on the left side of the chopper. During flight it was my duty to watch for aircraft from 90 degrees out back to our rear on my side; likewise for Tom on the other side. We always flew with the doors slid back, unless it was raining hellaciously. On occasion we would take one or two other people who requested to accompany us as "patient protectors." Their job was to provide any return fire should we be shot at while approaching, landing or taking off from the pickup zone, but it was mainly just an excuse for them to get a helicopter ride. However, in a hot LZ there is a critical period where the medic may be needed to provide covering fire during the initial lift off. This depended on how critical the patients just loaded were. Thus, "patient protectors" were useful during that time from takeoff to reaching altitude safe from gunfire. They sat in the backside seats and carried standard M-16 rifles, usually.

While departing our base (while stationed at Lai Ke our bases were: Quon Loi, Dau Tieng, or Lai Khe), the AC would make radio contact with the pickup party. We would ask the number of patients, the nature of their wounds (gunshot, shrapnel, accident, snake bite, burns, etc.), how many were ambulatory and how many on litters, were they American, ARVN, highlanders, civilians, POWs, etc. This way I would know how many litters to throw out as replacements for the ones being loaded on, how many IVs I might need to prepare, how much tape, and bandages to get ready, etc. and consider which medical facility or facilities we may need to go to. We also needed to know the nature of the LZ: was it "hot" or not? If we learned we'd be loading a "gunshot wound," that meant the enemy was nearby whereas "shrapnel wounds" usually meant mines, IEDs, or grenades, mortars, or artillery. We got as much detail as we could, and the AC would decide whether to request Cobra gunship cover or not. We would also find out if there were any fixed wing airplanes giving ground support. If so, we would need to coordinate with them to set our exact flight line to the LZ to avoid intersecting their flight patterns.

You do *not* want to fly through the wake turbulence of a jet. One time we went to pick up some ARVN wounded and after loading twelve wounded, another six unwounded ARVN climbed on board too. I had to throw others off the chopper so we could lift off. As we took off the AC complained that we were "maxed out" on the torque. He told the co-pilot to avoid any quick turns or ascents. "Take it nice and easy," he said. We lifted off slowly with 22 people on board. Others, anxious to leave the fierce battle below had grabbed our landing gear. My crew chief and I managed to pry them loose. We were gaining altitude, but slowly. We knew we were just a slow-moving target for the VC or NVA but somehow we didn't take any hits. At about 800 feet elevation, a jet swooped down in front of us and dropped some bombs. We flew right into the wake turbulence seconds after the jet had passed since we could not turn abruptly. It really threw us around. Fortunately no one fell out. The AC said we had maxed out the torque meter and wondered aloud how long we might keep flying. We made it all the way to the nearest base making an emergency landing on the runway. We had ambulances waiting to haul the wounded to the hospital. We did a shut down and Tom Cash went off to find someone to help him haul the chopper to a maintenance area for a top-level inspection. The AC, co-pilot, and I hitched rides back to Lai Khe while Tom stayed and worked on our chopper. Two days later we went and flew her back to Lai Khe.

Picking up on our "usual procedures," at the point of determining our flight line things were, theoretically, set. We would make radio contact and ask for smoke or, if it was night, a strobe light, to mark the LZ. Once the marker was located then it's just a matter of the approach.

In a hot LZ we would often approach at high speed at tree-top level and, once upon the LZ, make an abrupt stop, hover and set down. If the LZ was particularly tricky—if there was debris like blown trees on the ground so we could not land—the AC might take over flying the chopper from the co-pilot to do the hover. With hoist missions we would come down among and within the trees, in these cases the AC f lew the craft almost always. In a hoist mission, hovering too high to load patients, we would lower a hoist to haul up patients one at a time. With hoists we used either the "jungle penetrator," a torpedo-shaped object that unfolds to form a seat, or a wire-mesh litter for non-ambulatory patients.

Cold LZs allowed us to make a leisurely, standard approach. We'd land, the patients would be brought to us, usually, and we'd pull out our free litters and they'd load their loaded litters. The combat medic could tell me any particulars about any of the patients, especially those still in dire straits and not yet stabilized. Once loaded, I would check my side to be sure we were ready, look about to see if there were any obstacles, like trees or buildings, or cliffs, then say "clear left."

Once we took off from a secure LZ, I often took off my helmet to talk with the patients about their particulars. I looked over each patient quickly to decide who needed my attention first; indeed, that was often done while still loading the patients earlier. I would then deal with that situation, and if satisfied the patient was stable, move on to the next one. My mission was to keep the patients alive, not fix them. If I gave a patient morphine, I wrote an "M" on their forehead with a pen. For IVs I had saline and Ringer's Solution. We called these "blood volume expanders." A patient could lose so much blood that the veins begin to collapse. Adding an IV would increase the volume of blood and help prevent that.

We had the option to carry oxygen, but I ruled that out as too dangerous to the flight crew. Some medics carried them; I considered them a bomb waiting to explode the next time a bullet whizzed through the aircraft.

Burn patients were the most difficult. There was nothing I could do except use the Rule of Nines to estimate the amount of skin that was burned, the amount of burn, and relay that info to the hospital expecting us. (The Rule of Nines says that one leg equals 2/9ths of the person's skin; one arm equals 1/9th; the head equals 1/9th; the front torso equals 1/9th; and the back torso equals 1/9th.) Using this rule of thumb, I would report that 5/9ths of the person is burned, if they were burned on one leg, both arms, and the face. Hydration for burn patients lacking abdominal wounds was also important.

Sometime a patient needed my attention all the way in. In those cases, I'd ask Tom for some help with the others. Tom hated blood, but he never complained until after the mission. He was a real trooper when the need arose, which was often. We would land at the hospital LZ and offload the patients. I would relay any particulars to whomever looked like they were in charge on the ground. They would then give us cleaned litters to replace the ones we offloaded and we'd take off once the copilot heard "clear left" and "clear right." We would return to our base, letting the tower know of our approach, land, and shut down the chopper. Or, we would return for another pickup. Once landed, the AC and co-pilot filled out any logs they had then walked away, usually back to a poker game.

Tom and I still had a lot to do. We'd hook up the rotor to stabilize it, then I would clean up the medical messes in the chopper while Tom looked over "his baby" to ensure everything, and I mean everything, was alright. I then replaced any used materials with new ones. My last job was to then wipe down the windshield and polish it with a compound my crew chief gave me for that job. We would finish up together then go back to the RTO and check out the poker game and catch up on any news while we were gone. At night we stayed in the RTO because it was lit with a red bulb that protected our night vision should we be called out. Poker, crosswords, and letter writing were the main exercises. I sure wish they had Sudoku puzzles back then.

28   LOSING YOUR CHERRY

YOU'RE NOT REALLY CONSIDERED A DUSTOFF MEDIC OR Dustoff crew chief until you've lost your cherry—taken fire while picking up patients. Tom and I lost ours near Bu Dop, up near Quan Loi and Song Be. We went in and did a routine pick up of a superficial shrapnel wound. We took off and I patched him up. Everything seemed normal. But my crew chief Tom started acting squirrely. We dropped off the patient then shut down in our revetment. Tom got out and started looking over his baby. He knew something was wrong with *The Judge*. In two minutes he'd found it, or them. Two bullet holes, one in the tail and one in his right door. We always f lew with the doors slid all the way back, so it actually entered some area below the engine and behind us.

He told the AC that we were "Circle Red x" until he knew exactly what damage had been done that he couldn't inspect, and we ought to get the chopper back to Lai Khe, if they had a replacement. I knew that "Red x" for a Huey meant it couldn't fly at all. I never asked, but I assumed that a "Circle Red x" meant "go ahead and fly it, if you must." Then, the AC and the pilot came over and playfully dubbed us. I asked what the mock knighting ceremony was all about, and he said, "You've lost your cherry! You're no longer a virgin. You've been shot at!" He then went to the RTO shack and radioed for backup. Our replacement arrived in about two hours. It took a full day to repair the Judge.

You may have noticed I use phrasing like "pick up a shrapnel wound" instead of saying, "picked up a GI with a shrapnel wound." This comes from keeping radio chatter to a minimum. It's quicker to say, "I have two 70-percent burns and one gunshot wound to the stomach, over" than "I have two patients with 70-percent burns to head and body and one GI with a gunshot wound to the stomach, over." Fourteen words versus twenty-three, and the additional nine words add no additional needed information to the hospital receiving the message. Keep it short because others may need that radio frequency.

There was some kind of mission every day. I had heard about or seen pictures of all the wounds I was to treat while at Fort Sam. In Texas, I had shot an orange full of saline, set a splint on a mannequin, and watched a movie on mouth-tomouth resuscitation, and another on tracheostomies. When I left Fort Sam, I was a knowledgeable, theoretical, medic. Eventually, given enough time, a combat Dustoff medic will run into every conceivable medical situation. I was still working on my list; converting from a "medic in theory" to a practicing medic.

One day we approached a hot LZ and loaded on a GI with a face and jaw wound. Another GI had a gunshot wound to the leg. At takeoff in a hot LZ, my first priority was to help provide suppressing fire until we were out of gunshot range. At about 1,200 feet elevation or distance, I was able to check the patients. I checked the breathing and airway for the face-wounded GI. The airway was obstructed. I knew he needed a tracheostomy. I checked the other GI and told Tom to "press hard here" on the wound to curtail the blood flow. I went back then to get my other GI breathing again.

I thought back to the movie we'd watched in Fort Sam on this situation. No help. I knew what I must do: cut a hole through his windpipe into his throat below the voice box so that air could get to his lungs. *Remember: cut below the obstruction AND NOT INTO THE VOICE BOX.* It was now time to do just that, but I had nothing in my memory on how to do that. Then poof, 9th grade biology class popped into my mind: dissecting the frog! I remembered grasping the skin of the frog, pulling the skin tight with my thumb and forefinger, and drawing the scalpel along the skin to make the cut. Then, repeating until through. That all went through my mind in less than an instant, and I proceeded to clean the GI's throat, prepare my scalpel, grasp, and make the cut. I was astonished to see the tanned skin unzip and pure, white f lesh appear as I drew my scalpel across. I redrew the scalpel and cut deeper. With my fingers I could feel, then see, the cartilage rings of the throat, and I knew to cut between them. I was surprised there was no blood. I cut through and the patient gasped a huge breath! I put my finger in the hole to keep it from closing up and he started breathing regularly. I eventually took some rubber hosing, doubled it up to double the size of the opening and inserted it in the hole to keep it open. I then gave the guy an IV and cleaned up his wound as best as I could. I then leaned over and told him what was wrong with him, and what I had done to help him. His eyes were shut tight with swelling, so I don't know if he was alert or knocked out.

I checked Tom and our other patient to see how they were both doing. Tom really didn't like blood, especially if it wasn't his. But he was very intently holding back the blood flow from the gunshot wound. I clamped a small bleeding vessel and applied a pressure bandage. No bleeding, so I gave him an IV then re-checked the bandage: no bleeding still, so no danger; the patient would live to get to the hospital.

We dropped off the patients and then took off for another pickup. On the way to that second pickup we heard an unfamiliar voice on the radio. "Uh, Dustoff? You there?"

The AC replied, "This is Dustoff 48, go ahead."

"Uh, yeah . . . hello . . . I'm Doctor So-and-so, Chief Surgeon here at the hospital where you dropped off the facial wound. I just wanted to congratulate your medic for saving that man's life. The tracheostomy he did was fantastic. You'll let him know, won't you?"

Our helmets were all connected, so I heard him right there with the rest of the crew. Tom and I did a GI handshake (a "dap"). The co-pilot looked back and gave me a thumbs up.

Reflecting on it that night, it finally sank in that I had saved a life. That meant I could die tomorrow and the world would go on being affected by something I had done through the actions of that other person. It didn't matter what that person did, it wouldn't have happened without me being in the right place at the right time, with the right tools and knowledge. After that, I never had to prove myself to anyone, even to my own mind. I had, in my own eyes, achieved significance.

The next morning, I realized that Tom had saved a life too. I told him, and everybody else in the RTO an hour later that even though they all knew how much Tom hated blood, he had jumped right in, and without gloves put his hand on the wound and stopped the blood loss. "That saved that man's life," I said. "Thanks, Tom, for having my back."

29 EARLY DAYS AS A DUSTOFF MEDIC

AT FORT SAM OUR MEDIC TRAINING WAS MOSTLY theoretical. There weren't many hands-on experiences. There were lots of movies and mannequins. At the 36th Evac Hospital I had plenty of opportunity to watch the docs, nurses, and medics in the ER do their thing. I saw IVs implanted, cut downs done when the blood vessels had collapsed and you had to go in and search, with a scalpel, for a vein. I also learned that on guys, the fastest way to locate a vein when the vessels have collapsed is at the base of the penis. This knowledge saved a lot of time, and several lives, for the rapidity with which it could be done. We didn't need to apply anesthetic because the patient was already out cold, possibly even in shock.

The 36th Evac was also where I learned the names of all the tools I would eventually use. I learned by seeing them put in action. I even got to observe an autopsy once. This GI had come in with some shrapnel wound, fairly severe, but they got him cleaned of shrapnel and he was on the mend. But he told the nurse, and later his doctor, that he was going to die. They did all they could to calm him, but he fretted about it day and night. One morning the nurse found him dead in his bed. The docs called for an autopsy, thinking they had missed some piece of shrapnel, and if so, that would go on a report. I watched them cut him open and lay all his insides on the table, one part at a time. At this stage they were still investigating the cause of death and his body was treated as evidence. Lungs, heart stomach, liver all looked good. They started pulling out his small intestine and they found it full of black blood. Uh oh. "Internal bleeding," the doc said.

They searched every inch of the inside of the colon looking for a wound, and they eventually found it, in the large intestine. Upon close examination it turned out to be "ulcerative colitis" and a large bleeding sore had developed near some nerve cells (the doc pointed them out to us), which just happened to be next to a small artery.

The artery was ruptured, and no shrapnel was found when x-rays were taken "just to be sure." The doc said they don't know what causes these ulcers, exactly, but it was just bad luck that it formed right next to an artery. Once the artery ruptured the GI slowly bled out. The doc called it a "worry wart" since the patient had been fretting about his life for the past two weeks. "This patient literally worried himself to death," he told me.

I saw a lot of tools used during the autopsy, and techniques for slicing flesh without harming blood vessels. By the time I was with Lai Khe Dustoff it was assumed I was ready as a medic. But they had equipment I had to still familiarize myself with and figure out how to best employ it.

The first thing was my medic's bag.

I was told, "That bag needs to be ready the moment we crash and we run." So, the medic's bag was not for Dustoff patients but for us in the event we got shot down. Good to know! I obtained two sets of clamps, scissors, tweezers, bandages of all sorts, tapes of all widths, scalpels, and blades. One set for the chopper and our patients and one for the crew. There was also all the other stuff that's needed, like saline solution as a blood volume expander. I couldn't always get this so the hospital sometimes gave me bottles of Ringer's Solution. Then there was the morphine. I could only get ten ampules at a time from the hospital, but I kept them in my medic's bag because I figured if we crashed it would be a long time before we could get to a hospital and there would be the greatest need for pain relief. Besides, if I did need it in the chopper, it was available. Sharp scissors were essential for cutting away the clothing. The hospital cooks made sure we had aluminum foil, when available, to sharpen them on. But the best tool I had for cutting clothing was the foldable Buck Knife. I found this knife in the chopper one day while cleaning it after missions. I sawed the blade off so it was only an inch long, but it was always super sharp. I used it to slice through boot laces which otherwise always took time to remove so you could get to the foot.

Our work area in the chopper is shown in the following figure.

In the front (left in image) is the pilots' area. Behind them sat the medic and crew chief, one on each side. Flying empty we were located at the panel behind the pilots' door. The numbered areas indicate where we could load up to four litters. Behind that are some seats for either patient protectors (guys with guns) or walking wounded to sit. We were rated to carry, in addition to fuel and four crew, 2,200 pounds. As you can see, we could fit three seated passengers per side plus four litters. That's ten people. In a pinch we could fit in a 5th litter.

That's eleven people. The average weight of a GI in Nam was 166 lbs. plus, say 15 pounds of boots and fatigues. That's 1,191 pounds. So we still had room for a few extra people, if needed. The maximum we ever carried was 18, not including ourselves.

Inside the cabin there were several great cubbyholes where I stashed extras of everything.

On the way out to a mission, once we knew how many and the nature of the wound, my crew chief and I would set up a bunch of tape strips on the inside of our windowed panel. There were never enough tape strips though. With tape strips I could tape down bandages, tape the patient's IV feed lines and tape the forehead with a "M for morphine, and even in some cases tape slice wounds closed.

On occasion we would get a call that the wounded were in the deep forest. We'd ask if they had any means to chop down any trees. Except for the small LRRP teams, they always had some sort of explosive to blow a tree or two. A few units even had chain saws. In these situations we needed to install the hoist. That always delayed us a bit, but flying with it installed meant less room for wounded too. It was a bitch deciding which way to set up: hoist/no hoist. The hoist is always set up on the crew chief's side. During the hoist, the crew chief is the operator. There were two choices on what to lower: either the "forest penetrator" (a bullet-shaped device that had three arms that flipped down to sit on) or the Stokes Litter (a metal version of a litter). If a hoist had been needed, and the battle was ongoing, we would keep the hoist installed, and only remove it once the battle ended.

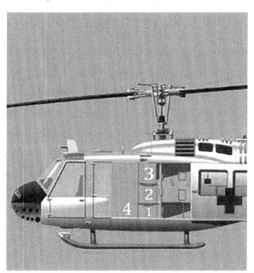

Dustoff cabin. Numbers show placement locations for four litters. Medic and crew chief occupied area behind the windowed panel between #4 and the pilot door. Up to four, but sometimes six, ambulatory patients could sit in the seats between Number 2 and the red cross.

Every hoist mission was unique. We wanted to get as low as possible, so often we would lower ourselves at a hover, turn the tail some, lower some more and maybe turn the tail again and

A Stokes Litter used in hoist missions.

come down some more. Often while hoisting up a patient we had trees right above us. This is how Randy Radigan got his nickname of "Rotorblades" from chopping his way down as much as he could. Most of the time the patients were not ambulatory, and most of the time a Stokes Litter was not available. In those case either the medic or the crew chief would go down to hold the patient on the way up with the other crew member running the hoist controls.

We were very vulnerable in these situations and we were always doing what we could to rapidly finish the mission and get some elevation.

Things didn't always work out that way.

30 BOTANY AND INVENTING

ON DAYS WHEN I WAS NOT ON 1ST or Second Up, I could relax. There was always the possibility of being called up to fly a Third Up mission if things got busy, so I had to remain nearby, within earshot of the siren. But I could relax. I did that by exploring the rubber tree plantation we were settled in behind our camp, if no sandbags needed filling. The Army loved setting up bases in rubber plantations. All the trees were in straight rows, evenly spaced, wide enough to drive a deuce-and-a-half truck between. A forest in formation and at attention: perfect. I was always interested in botany and there I had a chance to familiarize myself with the rubber trees.

"Botanizing" I called it. As I wandered around, I noticed that each tree's bark was marked with slanting linear scars, one below the next. I decided that each scar represented one harvest of sap. This was confirmed later when I came upon a tree with the sap ceramic collecting bowl about eight inches across, still attached. I got out my knife and cut the bark, watching as milky white sap oozed out and dropped into the bowl. Cool. I let it continue as I moved on, planning to return.

While botanizing I never watched where I was stepping. I was focused, looking for patterns, strange colors, and odd shapes. I was too busy checking out the fern growing on *that* tree, or wondering what kind of moss that was, and...what about *that feather?* I hadn't seen or heard any birds. Then, I was in it. The webbing stuck to my face and the brow of my cap. I stopped, then realized I had walked into a spider web that stretched from one rubber tree to the next. Even worse, from my perspective, my eye could see the entire surface of the web from me all the way to the tree. And in between was a huge spider gingerly making its way to me! The spider was as large as my hand.

I ran. I screamed. I continued running, imagining that the webbing was flowing behind me and the spider was hanging on and working its way to my head. I ran all the way to the road, about 150 yards. I flung my cap onto the ground and then quickly wiped myself clean of the webbing, sure that the huge spider was on me somewhere. I never found it. I learned later that it was probably the giant wood spider *(Nephila maculata)*. But right then I didn't care what its name was. My entire body shivered in one convulsive movement as if to rid my mind of this creepy thing.

Having gathered myself, I decided to head back. I was too far from base. I remembered I had to get the rubber bowl harvest, so I made my way back that way. As I botanized along the way, I was now also looking out for spider webs between trees. I came upon the bowl and it was nearly filled. Amazing! I took the bowl down and placed the remaining hardware in my fatigue pocket. I set the bowl down, grabbed some clean dirt, and placed it in the wound I had made in the bark in hopes the flow of sap might somehow coagulate and stop the bleeding. I then carried the bowl of sap back to my hooch and wondered what to do next. I remembered a company called Vulcanized Rubber Company from when I was growing up in Wilmington, Delaware. My dad had explained that they cooked the rubber, and this was called *vulcanization*.

With that memory, I decided I had to cook the sap. I set up our little stove and proceed to cook it using my mess kit. After a while it began to steam, then get sticky. Eventually satisfied it had cooked enough, I removed it and flipped the rubber onto the floor. It landed like a pancake. Cool. I touched it. It was hot, but not burning hot, and very sticky. I then gathered up the rubber pancake and began to fold it into a ball. It stuck to itself very well and with pressure from my hands became quite globelike. It ended up being a little larger than a baseball. I was very pleased with myself. I then took the "ball" and bounced it off the wooden floor. It bounced! It was a rubber ball! *I had made a rubber ball!* Cool. All my tentmates thought it was cool too. It gave us something else to do during the hours of waiting for a mission, until someone hit it with a stick and it got lost in the trees.

31 PEACEFUL SIGHTS

ONE DAY THIRD UP GOT A CALL TO make a flight to Cam Ranh Bay to deliver some paperwork. It was a long flight, mostly over the central highlands. These were beautiful mountains, mostly very green and seemingly unspoiled from our 2,000foot elevation. The sky was deep blue, the small puffy clouds gleaming white, and the cool air a great relief from the 95 degrees on the ground. There was no war during this flight. We landed the chopper and the AC and co-pilot took off on foot carrying envelopes. My crew chief, Tom, and I waited around, just passing the time and enjoying the sea air. The only thing I recall from that stay was the five large aircraft that flew over in a V formation. They seemed to be doing something, but I couldn't tell what. About ten minutes later there was this bitter taste in my mouth. I asked someone stationed there what just happened and he pointed out that there wasn't one green thing growing on the base. "That's because they spray it," he said. I thought nothing more of it once the bitterness in my mouth was washed out. Ironically, later I learned that the planes I'd watched had been spraying Agent Orange (AO).

Our pilots returned and we lifted off, went over to the POL (Petroleum, Oil, and Lubricants) depot and refueled, then headed out, southwest towards Lai Khe. We again flew over those verdant green mountains called the Central Highlands. I could look down and see all sorts of farming taking place. It wasn't rice farming; it was vegetable farming. The Da Lat area was known for its wonderful vegetables; even our hospital cooks got some in trades with other cooks. (Army hospitals got Navy rations, which were better than Army rations, so they always had something useful to trade.)

We were flying along with our doors slid back. I was sitting on my armor plate and right next to the open door. I loved that. I kept a watch out for aircraft but mostly had time to just gaze at the view: rolling green hills and majestic mountains and winding rivers. Suddenly, there, almost beneath us was a giant, and I mean very large, white sitting Buddha statue about 4/5ths of the way up a mountain. It was magnificent. I stared at it as long as I could. Just as it was almost out of sight, the co-pilot said, "Down there is Vietnam's only nuclear reactor." I was really surprised to hear that Vietnam had a reactor and I saw it as we passed. But I kept thinking about the Buddha. It was the coolest thing I had seen in 'Nam. In fact, on a scale of 1 to 10, most of 'Nam scored a -1 to 2, but the Buddha statue scored a 10. Fifty years later, my son and I found it, now covered in gold leaf.

My son, Mastin, and I in Vietnam, 2016 (Photo by Dylan Schmidt, used with permission)

32   R&R

EVERY ARMY GI SERVING IN VIETNAM, AT LEAST, was entitled to a 7-day Rest and Recreation (R&R) once a year in any one of several destinations in 1967-68: Hawaii, Tokyo, Hong Kong, Taipei, Manila, Bangkok, Singapore, Kuala Lumpur, and Sydney. Some of the destinations, like Sydney, required at least 10 months incountry before you would qualify. Many destinations required only three months in-country. The best part was that travel costs were covered. Married GIs met their wives in Hawaii. Those looking for bargains went to Hong Kong or Singapore.

Most GIs wanted to get laid, get drunk, and forget about the war, in that order. Therefore, most GIs went to Bangkok. One returning GI said, "The place is appropriately named: Bang Cock."

In all, I extended my tour two times. That entitled me to two 30-day leaves, and four seven-day leaves. The best part was that all transportation-related costs were reimbursable, as long as you had receipts.

I chose Bangkok the first time. During my first visit, I made a friend of a taxi driver and with a bellhop named Chon. They both took me places regular R&R GIs couldn't even find out about because they were outside the "permitted" areas allowed by the US Military. The Temple of Dawn was the best. It was my first upclose and in-person view of an Asian temple.

Then there was the Emerald Buddha (which is probably jade). It's a little over two feet tall and the stone has been carved into a sitting Buddha. Every three months they changed the clothes of the Buddha from one set of golden clothes to another, each representing the season just beginning. It was stunning.

I learned that Bangkok is a water-town. Canals stretch towards the city from every direction. The canals are about 3 feet wide and maybe two feet deep. People used very long, very narrow boats powered by outboard motors with very long

The Temple of Dawn, Bangkok, Thailand

extensions (10' to 15'!) for the propeller. Boats headed in different directions could pass, slowly and with care, in the narrow canals. Before sunrise, these canals were filled with boats loaded with garden harvests heading to the city markets. The Phraya River flows through Bangkok, and all these other rivers or canals connect into it. I walked along the river one morning and saw kids swimming, and mothers washing clothes. I looked down and saw trash floating in the water, and something larger. I stared at it, and the current turned the object and I could see it was the bloated belly of a dead dog. My interest in sightseeing the river walk ended there.

My bellhop friend Chon offered to take me to his "teacher" Khunkru. I jumped at the opportunity. We hopped into a taxi car and my friend gave directions. It was that ride that taught me that Thai taxi drivers use the horn as an invisible shield against oncoming traffic. Much to my dismay, it seemed to work. We went to the then-outskirts of town and our taxi pulled up to a magnificent, teakwood, raised house with an outstanding porch that went all the way around.

Inside, there were four rooms that I surmised, but I only entered two of them: the front area where you drop off your shoes and an overly large hall. The room was probably 20' x 20' and mostly bare. At one end, Chon's teacher, Khunkru, was with an old woman. They were sitting on chairs. There was a table, a flat-topped chest, and another chair. Behind him was a door and another room. On the far side of the room, near where we had entered, was a large, heavy, wooden throne. I was amazed to see spikes sticking out of every surface. As we walked by, I placed my finger on one of the spikes and pricked it. A small drop of blood flowed and I sucked it.

Chon introduced me to Khunkru. He smiled at me and returned his attention to the old woman. He placed his mouth on her left wrist and seemed to suck very hard. He reached to his mouth and pulled out a small round object, like a dull leadcolored BB. He placed it in a small bowl, then put his mouth on another part of her arm and sucked really hard. Again, he rolled another BB into his hand with his tongue. The woman looked at the teacher, smiled, stood up, said something in Thai, smiled again, turned and left. The Teacher then turned and looked at me, very intently. He then asked, in English if I would like a Coke! I said yes, though I am a Pepsi man. He took the small bowl with the BBs in his hand and rose to enter the door behind him. A moment later, he came back with a bottle of Coke with a straw in it. A small boy, maybe 6 or 7 years old, also came out and sat on the floor next to the Teacher. I saw the look of wonder in the boy's eyes. Maybe I was his first Caucasian. Then I glanced at my Coke and saw the straw was collecting air bubbles.

I knew shortly it would begin to rise, so I grabbed the boy's attention, then waved my hands very mysteriously, and pointed my fingertips towards the straw, and pretended to draw up the straw by my sheer will. The straw suddenly lifted upwards a tad, and I, with a broad smile on my face lowered my hands and put them in my lap, completely pleased with my magic show.

The kid then stood up, walked over to my Coke, placed his hands above it, with fingers pointing down, and did the same thing! The straw bobbed up another notch and the kid slapped his hands as if getting the dust off them, looked at me with a big smile of accomplishment and, sat down next to the Teacher. "My son has seen this!" said Khunkru, smiling.

Chon then explained to the Teacher that I was interested in Buddhism, plants, history, and that I flew on a helicopter in Vietnam "as a soldier." Khunkru then asked me if I knew any Buddhist prayers. "No," I replied.

He said, "I will teach you one. It's Sanskrit, very holy." The prayer, phonetically, went like this:

Kố phat, kố phat, kam sur At BuddHA, (rising tone) *Kố phat, kố phat, kam sur At BuddHA,* (rising tone)

-then a pause-

Kố phat, kố phat, kam sur At BuddHA, (lowering tone, and "Buddha" is said a little slower.)

I have no idea what it means, but he said this prayer is one of respect that you say when you enter a Temple and face the Buddha statue. You first light three sticks of incense and place them between your fingers of both hands held in a prayer-like position. You then say the prayer at the same time while moving your hands up and down with the cadence, head bowed in respect, not worship. All while on your knees.

He then went on to say that Buddha was a man, not a god, and that the best we could hope for was to be as much like the man Buddha had been as possible. "You are not praying to Buddha. You are respecting and honoring what he became, as . . . a . . . man, and trying to be same." It was a stunningly elegant lesson. I knew enough history about the Crusades and the Reformation to realize that this did not seem to be the kind of belief system to attract the power- hungry, who always, it seems, want to place themselves between you and your God.

He then mentioned that he noticed I had given his throne chair a close look. I asked him if he really sat in it. He got up, took off his over-robe so he only had on his sarong. He walked over to the chair, leapt onto it and sat down, grasped the ends of the hand holds, and shifting his body from his waist to his head and shoulders, rocking, he noisily flung the throne chair all about the room! Now understand, his feet were pressed down on the spikes, his back, the back of his head, the underside of his arms, the back of his calves and, his bum were all in contact with these sharp metal spikes. The only part of his body not in contact with the spikes was where he grasped the hand holds. In addition, spikes were pointed at his sides and ribs too. He rolled and jostled the spiked throne all around the room in a huge circle, until he stopped near where he started. It took maybe 90 seconds. When he stood up, he was standing on the spikes that were beneath his feet. Every flat surface had spikes, lots of spikes, hundreds of spikes. They were about one-half inch apart. He stepped off the spikes and onto the floor, came over and offered himself for inspection. There were no cuts or punctures anywhere, including the bottoms of his feet. I was mystified. My memory of the rest of the visit, and the rest of my time in Bangkok after that is a complete blank.

I returned to Lai Khe safely. There I was again on First Up and flew lots of missions. One of the missions was a call that a general had been wounded and needed evacuation. We went in and picked him up. The general was ambulatory and I remember him jumping into the chopper. Apparently, he was flying circles around a ground action, giving orders, when his chopper was shot down. He was now sitting in the back of our Dustoff when, over my helmet intercom, I heard the pilot, who was looking back, telling me to "do something."

"Like what?" I asked.

"I dunno," said the pilot. "Give him an IV." I turned toward the general, pulled out a litter, opened it, and invited the general to lie down on it. He grinned a big grin and did so. I then took his left arm, pulled up the sleeve, and stuck him with my IV needle. I turned on the IV to drip as little as possible. We offloaded him at the surgical hospital where other VIPs were already waiting for him. They saw him on a litter, with an IV, and they looked worried. He was carried in his litter to a Jeep and carted to the hospital. It was a good show and, the only time I got to stick it to a general.

I'm sure he got a Purple Heart for that, possibly a CIB (Combat Infantryman Badge) as well.

33 MISSING BIRDS

THE ONLY TIME I REMEMBER SEEING BIRDS IN Vietnam was once on a mission up to the Fish Hook, on the Cambodian border. We were flying along at about 2,500 feet ASL. We were listening to radio Saigon when all of a sudden Thtr-thtr-thtterthterrt-thtter-thitter-thunk!

Several birds found themselves trapped in the windshield wipers. Other than that, we were fine. I never saw birds while on the ground. Though I did find that one feather once in the plantation at Lai Khe.

I still wonder what happened to them all.

34 POKER, ANYONE?

IT WAS A DULL EVENING IN LAI KHE. Dusk was coming fast; the night was cool and calm.

The big social event of the night was coagulating in the radio room (RTO). "Flashlight" Johnson was at the radio and Randy Radigan was leaning over the counter that separated them. I came in and joined in, listening to the radio chatter. Later a few others came in and talk began to gravitate around a future poker game and who owed who.

Flash-Bam!

Stunned silence. We looked around at each other lying on the floor. We heard nothing outside. Randy crawled over and turned off the lights, while others from outside came crawling into the RTO. Randy took charge. We each had our own issued (and unissued) weapons that we either kept with us or in a chopper—they were never too far away. Randy ordered a perimeter set up around the RTO. Then he jumped the radio dial to the 3rd Brigade (1st Infantry Division) radio frequency only to find silence. He tried to raise anyone to no avail. *That was scary.*

I was utterly bewildered. After the blast, the entire Lai Khe camp was dark and silent. But no gunfire. Chatter turned to sappers—VC sneaking into the base with explosives. They were silent boogeymen creeping around on any dark corner with death in their heart. Randy said something about a nursery rhyme, he was trying to recall which one. "What?!" I asked.

Randy said, "The secret frequency is encoded in a nursery rhyme. But I can't recall which one; give me some nursery rhymes!" So there we were, scared shitless, trying to remember nursery rhymes—reciting them for him. "No, not that one, give me another," he went on. "Come again? No."

Someone said "Jack be nimble . . ."

"That's it!" whispered Randy excitedly. Somehow this was the code. He told Flashlight to dial 913.916. Suddenly we heard chatter on the radio. We quickly found out that no one knew what had happened. No one!

Flash-Kaboom!

Another blast, but that blast was right off of our perimeter. With guns, grenades, and knives we redoubled our perimeter defense around the RTO shack. After a few more minutes, Randy turned the lights back on and stuck his head out the door and shouted, "It's alright boys!" in a high-pitched voice and continued, "You can come out noooowwww!"

It took us three hours to metabolize all that adrenaline. Too nervous to pick up that poker game, we hung around the radio for a while trying to figure out what happened. It turned out a couple of guys in the Armor unit decided to take a tank out for a joy ride along the perimeter, and, of course, they had to fire a couple of rounds.

Later the action moved outside to the choppers: stargazing, some pot smoking, and chatter.

35   DEFYING A GENERAL'S ORDER

THE BU DOP, LOCH NINH, SONG BE AREA was close to the Cambodian border and the Ho Chi Minh Trail. It was part of our area at the Quan Loi station. Often our stay there was uneventful, but just as often, fighting would erupt and we would be kept busy. On September 13, 1968, heavy fighting broke out and all of a sudden, our hearts game came to an end. We took off and discovered that we had about fifty wounded in several areas that needed immediate evacuation. Several hours of moving wounded didn't seem to relieve the pressure. We *still* had fifty casualties waiting for pickup.

During the fighting, the commanding general of the 1st Infantry Division, Maj. Gen. Keith Lincoln Ware, a Medal of Honor recipient from WWII, was killed. His immediate subordinate took command and got on the radio and called us. He told us to quit what we were doing and come down and pick up the dead general's body and take it back to Loch Ninh. Randy Radigan, our AC, asked if the general was dead and the reply was, "Yes, now get your butt moving." Randy replied that he understood the situation but that he had about fifty wounded still to move. The radio blasted back that moving the dead general was more important. Randy replied that he had wounded to go pick up and that the dead general would have to find another way back.

"Dustoff 41, I am *ordering you!*" came back the radio. Randy replied that moving the wounded was our mission. He then stated that he was refusing to remove the body. The general replied that this was in defiance of a direct order.

Randy, very coolly, said, "Sir, I am an Aircraft Commander. You do not have the authority to 'order' me." The general on the radio then asked for his name, rank and serial number, which Randy provided.

The general then said, "So, if I can't order you, who can?"

Randy replied, "No one in Vietnam can, Sir, not even (the theater commander) General Westmoreland. If you get the President or the Secretary of Defense to order me, I will."

"Goddamn you," the general replied.

"Sir," the AC said, "I'm sorry to be blunt, but moving a body is a supply problem, not a medical problem. I've got living men to go pick up, and that's my mission." The general never replied.

Much later that night, after all the hauling was done and we were back in the RTO shack at Quan Loi waiting for another mission, we were playing poker with the red light on to protect our night vision. The RTO got a call; someone was asking to speak with Dustoff 41. Being right there, Randy picked up the mic and said, "Go ahead, this is he."

"This is the 1st Infantry Division Surgeon, Maj. General (I don't recall his name)." "Yes?" said the AC.

"I called to say that you made the right call today about General Ware. You spoke with the second in command, and they were close friends. That's all I've got to say. Good night," and he hung up.

36   LOW LEVEL

SOMETIMES I WASN'T PROUD OF MY OWN PEOPLE, like during the sandbagging party back at Vung Tau. One day a chopper had come up from Saigon to make a blood delivery. While in the radio room, we received a call that that chopper was needed to make another pick up at Saigon and deliver it to Lai Khe. However, there wasn't a rush, as the package had not yet arrived at the 3rd Field Hospital in Bien Hoa, near Saigon yet. The pilot asked around the room if anyone wanted to go to Saigon "for a bit." I volunteered. I was running out of cigarettes and needed to pick up a few cartons at the Px. Another member of our team volunteered in order to pick up some beer and a bottle of Four Roses Bourbon. So we went. When we got there, the AC asked if the package was ready yet. He was told, "Wait." He looked at us two passengers and said, "Go." So we made it to the Px.

I was stunned to learn that the only cigarettes available were Carltons. "What are those?" I asked myself. I normally smoked Pall Malls, the long, unfiltered ones. They were like Camels, only better. As a nicotine addict, I bought the Carltons anyway, four cartons. My pal found there was no beer because the VC had sunk the ship in the Saigon River before delivering the beer.

But he did manage to get a bottle of Four Roses, which I found out later was about as good as my Carltons. We made it back to the helipad and the package arrived about forty-five minutes later. I learned later it turned out to be promotion orders for some physician at our surgical hospital.

Off we went, up and heading north-west at about 500 feet and climbing. We crossed the "Saigon." (Actually, it was the Dong Nai River, but every river near Saigon was called the Saigon). The crew chief—not my crew chief Tom—grabbed one of his medic's IV bottles and tried to bomb some people in a sampan. I was horrified and, much to my shame later, did nothing. He laughed, but all I could think about was, *What if he hit someone?*

The flight to Lai Khe is basically one of following Highway 13, the only way North out of Saigon. Pilots love to "low level," i.e., fly about 50 feet off the ground, especially when no one of higher rank is watching. Remember, most of the pilots and ACs were about 19-21 years old, still not old enough to rent a car in the US or vote. So there we were, low-levelling along Highway 13, buzzing everyone along the road. The AC pointed out some cows up ahead and the co-pilot maneuvered over to the field, coming down real low, probably about 25 feet off the ground. He headed right for the cows, which bolted from the herder, an old man, and gave the chopper crew something to laugh about. Luckily, the pilot saw the trees up ahead and pulled up on the collective, and back on the stick, just in time to miss the trees. We lowlevelled all the way to Lai Khe.

When we landed, as usual, the chopper's crew chief got out and inspected his craft. He pulled part of branch from the right front skid and showed it to the co-pilot. We all knew then just how close we had come to the trees.

I have recalled this incident many times since then. It was no way to win the hearts and minds of the locals; something MACV (Military Assistance Command Vietnam) never got across to the ground troops. But as still a teenager, well, actually I was 20 then, the low-levelling was fun.

37 COFFEE BREAK AT FIRE BASE RITA

THE 4TH PLATOON HAD SIX HELICOPTERS. WE WERE expected to have four of them ready at all times. One was usually down for repairs, for either the 25-hour Inspection (flight hours 25, 50, and 75 after the 100-hour inspection) or the 100hour Inspection. Crew chiefs were each assigned a helicopter. It was their chopper, not the co-pilots or the AC's, but theirs. They either performed or oversaw all the maintenance of their chopper. There was a another inspection, of which I know little, other than that was the one where they took off the "Jesus Nut" that held the rotor blades in place. It was called the "Jesus Nut" because if it ever came off during flight that's who everyone would see next. I recall one crew chief who said he would call it the "Fuck" nut. He said, "Because that's what I would say after it came off: FUCK!"

So with (usually) four choppers in use, we kept two at Lai Khe, a "First Up," and a "Second Up." Second Up would go out on missions if First Up was already out on a mission. Otherwise, all the missions that day belonged to First Up. We also sent one chopper to Dau Tieng (halfway to Tay Ninh) and one to Quan Loi, all the way up Highway 13 past An Loc in a rubber plantation near the Cambodian border. Both of these extension sites had medical facilities to drop off patients, so they were (usually) self-sufficient. The usual stay was three days or when the 25 flight hours were nearly used up, whichever came first.

After sunset one evening October 31st, 1968 we got a call while at Quan Loi to pick up some wounded at a firebase, Fire Support Base (FSB) Rita, an artillery base a few hundred yards from Cambodia and the Ho Chi Minh Trail.

It was important to know the kinds of wounds in advance. Gunshot wounds meant the enemy was possibly still near. In those cases, Dustoff could call for fixed-wing cover, Cobra gunship cover, and/or artillery fire (if available) to distract the

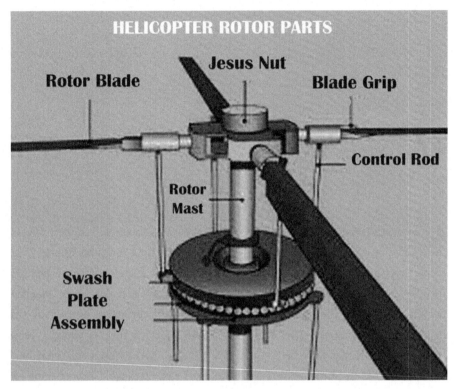

Location of the Jesus Nut and the control rods. Note: This a four-bladed chopper image, unlike the Hueys we flew, which had two blades.

enemy while our unarmed Dustoff (ordered by the Geneva Convention) made the extraction. Note: Not all "Medevacs" are "Dustoffs," even though both are used to extract wounded. Medevacs were a creation of the 1st Armored Cavalry and were armed with .50 cal. machine guns; Dustoffs were unarmed and came under the Geneva Conventions.

This time the wound was "shrapnel." There was no additional detail. On the way out, the AC and pilot had a discussion with the helipad RTO (Radio Telephone Operator) about being sure to get details when it comes to "shrapnel." Shrapnel could be from a mine (or in today's language, an IED), or it could be from mortar fire, which, like gunshot wounds, could mean the enemy is still nearby. Knowing if the enemy was still nearby was important.

When we arrived, the base was under heavy mortar attack. There were more wounded since they first called it in. We took them all and made for the hospital at Quan Loi. While we were unloading patients at the helipad, FSB Rita called to say there were more wounded to come pick up. Our AC got on the radio and asked for cover from anyone who could provide it.

Everyone was busy elsewhere that night, so no cover. But somehow, later a Spooky gunship showed up. It was dark and there was this plane flying around putting out 5,000 rounds a minute onto the enemy positions.

During that pickup, a firefight erupted along one part of the perimeter. We could see the red tracers going out and the green tracers coming in. US-made tracers were red. Chinese tracers were green. It was a ground attack. Plus mortar fire. We were a slow-moving, unarmed target with a big bull's eye pasted on us. But we landed and picked up more wounded, including gunshot wounds. Then we headed back. There was no let up all night. About 4 AM we landed at our usual spot and the Rita RTO informed us that that part of the base had been overrun and was now in enemy hands. We had landed in enemy territory. My crew chief and I were armed and ready to defend the chopper, but we were not fired at. Our chopper jumped up, and moved over to where our people were. The guys helping load the wounded looked tired, but determined.

When we got back to the LZ at Quan Loi, I told one of the medics hauling off the wounded to go wake up the cook and have him prepare a full ewer of fresh coffee. Then we hauled more wounded back and forth from FSB Rita. Later, near dawn, at the hospital LZ, that medic I'd spoken with earlier wheeled up a full 100-cup ewer of coffee! I was surprised and delighted. On the way back to FSB Rita, I balanced the ewer carefully so it didn't tip. When we landed, I offloaded the ewer for the ground troops, then loaded on more wounded. No time lost. I saw GIs carrying away the ewer as we lifted off. I remember the crew chief saying the chopper was whistling.

We continued hauling wounded until after day break, when, finally, no more calls came in. Fifty years later, I learned that one of the patients we took on was later awarded the Medal of Honor for his actions that night: Major General (then LTC) Charles C. Rogers.[2]

---

[2] A small part from his MOH citation reads: "In the early morning hours, the fire support base was subjected to a concentrated bombardment of heavy mortar, rocket and rocket propelled grenade fire. Simultaneously the position was struck by a human wave ground assault, led by sappers who breached the defensive barriers with Bangalore torpedoes and penetrated the defensive perimeter. Lt. Col. Rogers with complete disregard for his safety moved through the hail of fragments from bursting enemy rounds to the embattled area. He aggressively rallied the dazed artillery crewmen to man their howitzers and he directed their fire on the assaulting enemy."

Once the battle ceased, we returned to Quan Loi. Tom Cash, my crew chief, checked the chopper. He found three bullet holes in the rotor blades and filled them with chewing gum to keep them from whistling. He wrote notes in his logbook. He then informed us that his chopper now needed a 25-hour Inspection. We called Lai Khe and got a chopper to come up and relieve us. Once we got back, Tom climbed up on his chopper and began doing whatever crew chiefs do during a 25-hour inspection. Then I heard him yell, "Damn! Doc, come look at this!" he ordered. (Every medic was called "Doc" by his crew chief, as well by our last names.)

When I climbed up, he showed me a metal rod that controls the lift angle of one of the rotor blades. (See picture above, arrows.) There was a bullet hole clear through it, with similar amounts of metal on either side still holding it together. He took it off and it became a "9-Day Wonder" in the RTO shack, an oddity everyone wanted to see. If that rod had failed, we would have lost control and lift on the rotor blade and crashed.

Forty-nine years later, I met one of the people from FSB Rita that night at the 100th Anniversary Reunion of the 1st Infantry Division in Kansas City, and learned more details from an account of the battle by David H. Puckett, Sr., Honorary Sergeant Major of the Regiment.[3]

Fire Support Base Rita had been manned about three months earlier by the 1/4 Cavalry of the 1st Infantry Division, known as "the QuarterHorse," to provide perimeter support for artillery attempting to block a major infiltration route into War Zone C from Cambodia. The artillery units providing support out of Rita were six 105mm towed howitzers of B Battery, 1st Battalion, 5th Artillery, and six 155mm self-propelled howitzers of C Battery, 8th Battalion, 6th Artillery. From mid-October the FSB had been the target of daily and nightly mortar and rocket attacks. The 1st Battalion, 16th Infantry (Mech) had been providing perimeter defense for the base as well as running local patrols and search and destroy missions. On November 1st, [1968] an estimated battalion of NVA launched a ground attack against Fire Support Base 'RITA.' During the battle the perimeter was breeched and the Commanding Officer ordered red flares and everyone to "fix bayonets."

The artillery started firing antipersonnel rounds horizontally. By dawn the enemy had been repulsed. The fellow I talked to was there that night. I asked him if he remembered the hot coffee. He did, had wondered about it, and thanked me for it! Cool.

---

[3] Read more at: www.4thcavassoc.org/pg4ff.htm.

38 "THAT'S NOT INCOMING, THAT'S ARTILLERY"

ONE TIME AT QUAN LOI WE WERE WITH a new co-pilot who had just joined the unit. His name was Mr. Plume, so we called him "Feather." He eventually became an AC with call sign Dustoff 42, but that was later.

My Crew Chief, Tom, was worried about his chopper, and after talking with the AC, they both decided to call Lai Khe Dustoff to check on something. That left Feather and me alone at our chopper. From previous experience I knew that the 175mm cannons were down at our end of the runway, back behind us. They started firing and Feather jumped a mile. I said, "Nah, that's not incoming, that's artillery." I wanted to assure him there was nothing to worry about. After all, he was the FNG. I smiled knowingly.

We continued sauntering away from our chopper towards several piles of PSP, interlocking steel planking used to create the runway. One of the piles was nearly depleted and it looked like a good place to sit and watch the activity on the runway while we waited for the rest of our crew to return. The artillery continued to fire. We finally reached the PSP and turned to sit when all of a sudden, an explosion occurred in the middle of the runway. It was incoming mortar fire! We could see a series of plumes caused by just-exploded mortars going away from us.

Charlie always seemed to send mortars in a line. I instantly realized the VC were "walking" mortars down the Quan Loi runway, toward us! It wasn't our artillery firing at all! We dashed between the tall piles of PSP for protection. I was embarrassed as hell. Just then, Feather turned and asked me, "Are you sure that was artillery fire we heard earlier?" I looked over and the guns were silent. After that, I no longer thought of any FNG as anything other than a vet.

39 GENERAL THOUGHTS ABOUT FNGS

THE THING ABOUT FNGS IS THAT EVERYONE IS one when they first arrive. Rank is irrelevant. But, the new recruits, as opposed to "lifers" coming in from another assignment, were the worst. They had no idea what to expect. Their doe eyes said it all: naïve, aware they were near danger, and clueless as to what to do if something happens.

I remember when Major Basil Smith arrived. He was a stocky, well-built man, and pretty lean. After he noticed that several of us had mustaches, he announced a rule: only people who ran the four-mile block in the center of the rubber plantation could keep their mustaches. Of course, we all decided right there and then, that no major was going to take away our mustaches. The Army had given us a right to have them, and have them we would. So, every day, before breakfast mess, we all went out, led by Major Smith, and ran the four roads, each a mile long, that formed the internal center square of Lai Khe Base. We did this for a week. After our run one day, Major Smith said, "No more running. Everyone can keep their mustaches, so long as they are neatly trimmed." He turned and walked away. We looked at each other, did the GI handshakes all around, and felt we had won. Months later, Major Smith told me over coffee one night that he had done that to create "unit cohesion." Using his psychology degree, he'd decided that this was a good way to 1) introduce himself and, 2) build up the cohesion of a bunch of relative FNGs who hadn't worked long enough together to bond. It worked.

After our four-mile runs with Major Smith ended, he called me into his personal hooch to talk to me about being "in-country." He said my file showed I had been in country more than most, and he wanted me to "keep an eye on him" and come to him if I ever saw him doing things, or giving orders, that I thought were putting the unit, or individuals, in needless danger.

He asked me not to mention this conversation to anyone and I agreed. As it turned out, I never had any need to say anything to him; however he did refuse a mission once and that pissed a lot of us off, but I never learned the details of that. Since our conversation happened 50 years ago, I think I can talk about that conversation now.

For enlisted men, seeing FNGs was a temporary mood booster. Misery loves company and it's nice to see someone who has more misery ahead of them than me. Plus, they are fun, and easy to pull pranks on. As an FNG, I got sent to get a "board stretcher," "rotor wash," "short circuits," "grid squares," the "eye-dee-ten-tee" manual (ID-10-T manual), and get a 100 yards of some "flight line." These requests only work for a short while. Soon the FNG gets wise and actually starts to *think* about what he's being asked to do.

So, for any clueless civilians, here are the definitions for these "requested items":
- Board stretcher: no such thing; you can't stretch a board
  (but you can bend them).
- Rotor wash: That's the wind created by a helicopter rotor when it spins.
- Short circuits: Burned out electrical circuits.
- Grid squares: These are the grids found on military maps to provide
  distance and coordinate information.
- The ID-10-T Manual: This spells "idiot." 'Nuff said.
- Flight line: This is the place at an airport where the planes and choppers
  are kept when being repaired or waiting for missions.

40 DUSTOFF LESS THAN A MEDEVAC

EVERY US TROOP THAT ARRIVED IN VIETNAM NOTICED the dust. It was more noticeable out in the field and away from paved runways. The clay in my part of Vietnam (III Corps) was laterite. It's red. In the dry season it's hard; during the wet season it's hard and slippery. Laterite was pretty good for constructing "temporary" runways. If it became permanent and a General was nearby, it often became paved with PSP (perforated steel plating, less well known as a Marston Mat). But PSP (see figure) is perforated, and the laterite below a PSP runway still creates dust. There was dust everywhere.

Helicopters were nearly ubiquitous for GIs in 'Nam. The wop-wop-wop told you one was nearby. The kind of wop-wop-wop told you what kind of chopper it was: a Huey, a Chinook, a Sikorsky Sky Crane, a Loach, or a Cobra were the ones I mostly saw and heard. When a chopper landed near troops, they were always 'dusted off' by the chopper's rotor wash. In 1963, Major Lloyd E. Spencer, Commander of the U.S. Army 57th Medical Detachment (Helicopter Ambulance) used the term "Dustoff" as his call sign for medical evacuations. The term stuck. From then on, dedicated medical evacuation helicopters used the call sign Dustoff followed by a number that indicated the AC (Aircraft Commander) piloting the chopper. They became known as "Dustoffs" and were unarmed air ambulances under the Geneva Convention. The 1st Air Cavalry Division had Medevacs, also marked with red crosses but they carried 50 cal. machine guns and designated door gunners. I never considered them part of Dustoff because they didn't seem to follow the rules of the Geneva Convention that "ambulances" (air or ground) must be unarmed. I also don't know if they ever used the Dustoff call sign. The Medevacs were organic to the Division, whereas Dustoffs were under the command of the 44th Medical Brigade.

A perforated steel plated (PSP) runway, otherwise known as a Marston Mat

41 THE CLUBHOUSE

IT WAS PROJECT DAY. WE HAD JUST FINISHED building our hooches. They were six-man tents set up on plywood floors elevated about two feet above the ground. We'd also worked on our bunkers, and they were designed so that if we were in our cots we could make it into the bunker bolt hole in about three steps. We had steps going down about eight feet, and we had three feet of sandbags over head. We had run electric wires in from the generator so we had power for our phonograph player to play the one album we had, *Sgt. Pepper's Lonely Hearts Club Band*. One of the crew chiefs, Steve Huntley I believe, who "owned" Iron Butterfly (the chopper), had obtained some iridescent posters. We put a blue bulb in the light socket and had ourselves a mini hippie den right in the middle of Lai Khe. We often went down to smoke pot and listen to our one Beatles album, over and over and over.

So the hooches and bunkers were done. We had built ourselves a shower. Every day we ran the tanker truck over to the Lai Khe water station, filled it up, then in the morning we took cold showers from it. On this day, one of the ACs, I believe it was Captain Owens, pulled in with a recovered jet plane fuel tank. It had been jettisoned by the plane and could not be reused. It was aluminum and held 450 gallons. We cleaned it out as best we could, then cut some holes in it on one side and placed two US Army emersion kerosene heaters in it. See inset.

The round cylinder at the top right held the kerosene. It is allowed to drip down to the bottom doughnut-shaped area where it is lit and burns. The fire heats the water down at the doughnut area and the exhaust went up and out the chimney.

Once we got it hooked up we tried it out. We discovered the hot water rose and the cold water stayed at the bottom. So, once it was operational, we had the RTO operator go out at 4 AM to turn on the heaters, then come back at 5:30 am to stir the water. When the rest of us woke up we had hot showers. We already had re-built the clubhouse (formerly a warrant officer's hootch, then sold to Sp5 Mike Casper, one of our crew chiefs for 20 bucks, then commandeered by Maj. Smith for the officers, but never used) out of leftover boards from here and there and we'd repaired and repurposed the old blood chiller so we could have cool beer when the generator was running. It was not an *officer* club, or an *enlisted* club, it was The Clubhouse. Everyone came to the Clubhouse.

Anyone could come and partake. We usually had canned sodas, or "pop," on hand. There was this older supply NCO, who had less rank than he should have for his age, who decided to "run" the Club. We'd go in and say, "I'll take a soda pop." He always replied, "Don't call me 'Pop,'" which was, if anything, an invitation to call him Pop. So, we always did, since the "soda" was a "soda pop" too. It all boiled down to whether there was a comma or not. By now, we had pretty much fancied up our place as much as it was gonna get: hot showers, cool beer, our music listening place. All we needed were more albums.

In September 1968, I was preparing to celebrate my 365 days in Vietnam with my Dustoff buddies. I copped a ride down to Saigon, went to the Px and bought, along with my cartons of cigarettes, a bottle of vodka and a bottle of Four Roses. The reason for the helicopter flight was "to pick up some orders," but the real reason was to pick up a half palate of beer. We returned from Saigon and offloaded the liquids. This time the beer was Carling Black Label.

While 1st and Second Up were in the RTO room—officially the "Ready Room" with a red light bulb on after dark to protect the crew's night vision—the rest of us had finished dinner mess and eventually wandered one-by-one over to the club. I was there early and started drinking whisky-coke, a half glass of coke, (though it may have been Nehi or Tab) with the Four Roses to top it off and eating fresh corn on the cob brought to us by our hospital cook who had traded some Navy rations for it from a hospital cook near Da Lat. It was a great time, but I don't remember many details. Most of the way through the evening I finished the Four Roses and started on the vodka with Coke. My only memory of that part of the party was my speaking above the noise of the crowd saying, "I've got three things I want to say," while looking at Chief Warrant Officer Marler. I recall saying that three or four times. After that it's all black.

When I woke up, I was in my cot, in my tent. I felt awful. My mouth was dry like cotton, and my head swirled. I laid there for a while, then turned a bit in the cot. I felt like I was in a mudhole. I eventually got myself together and sat up in my cot.

I was soaked. And I stank. I stood up and liquid poop started running down my fatigues onto my legs. I had shit and peed myself in my sleep. Damn. I coaxed myself to walk to our outdoor shower area and turned on the water, it was sort of warm. I stripped, saw the mess in my underwear, and just stood under the falling water. I had a serious beard on my face. I got myself clean and my clothes clean enough to give to my mama san (a local woman who was our tent maid) to wash. I walked back to my tent naked, hiding myself with my soaked fatigues. I got dressed, then took my cot outside and spent an hour cleaning it. Then I cleaned the floor under my cot. I then shaved and re-dressed and considered myself presentable. Outside I met CWO Marler. He asked how I was, and then told me I had been out for two whole nights. It was now the third day after my celebration. He laughed about how he'd helped me make it back from the clubhouse to my cot. "You were planting corn all along the way," he said, referring to the corn on the cob we'd had for dinner.

That's all I remember about my "party."

I reflected later about my "absence" from reality as I slept off my hard drinking. I had finished one and a half quarts of Four Roses and vodka, plus some beers. I was told I had been "blind drunk" and kept raving about having three things to say, but they never could get me to say what those three things were. And I have no memory of what they were either. Three people helped me back to my cot that night. I was out for 53 hours, more or less. There was nothing going on in my head during that time; I was out. Zero. No dreams, no thoughts, nada. Black midnight. I imagined that must be what it's like when you're dead. I concluded later that it was just like before I was born and settled on the idea that when you die, you go back to where you were before you were born. That's not so bad.

I never feared death after that, and I couldn't get near strong alcohol for about ten years.

Even now, when I smell strong alcohol, even my favorite cognac, I remember that morning.

42 LIMA BEAN PANCAKES

IN ANOTHER DRINKING INCIDENT A MONTH EARLIER WE had an all-night poker game. One of the players was the cook from the neighboring surgical hospital. About 4 AM he said he had to leave and wondered if someone could help him find his way. We all put our cards down and escorted him to the kitchen as a group. While on our way, we convinced him he should make blueberry pancakes for breakfast. It took us a while to get there, even though the whole trip was only about 100 yards. With him delivered we returned to our tent and continued the game. By this time we were out of everything but pop.

Finally it was 6AM, time for breakfast. We got up and walked over. It was lighter and we could see our way with no problem. We walked in, got our trays, and proceeded to

Army food cans for Meat & Beans (left) and Biscuit Mix (right)

fill it. There they were, blueberry pancakes! I loaded up with five of them and poured syrup on top, and in between them too. Once seated I dug into the pancakes. After several bites I actually looked at my food and couldn't find any blueberries. I looked closer and then I saw green things. I dissected my top pancake and extracted a whole lima bean. Army food cans look pretty much the same, unless you read the number, especially if you are drunk. Actually, lima bean pancakes are okay, if you have a lot of syrup on them.

43 WHATS GROSS

MOST PEOPLE DON'T KNOW WHAT GROSS IS. TO some it's a meal too cold, to others its lima bean pancakes, and for others it's the smell of an untidy bathroom. With respect to what is truly gross, these are delights.

One of the goals of military training is to teach soldiers not to panic when faced with life- threatening situations. It is during those times that you need to keep your cool and think your way out of the situation and not just react. But the military training does not prepare soldiers for when they encounter horror. Horror is the feeling of revulsion that can happen after experiencing something frightening or deeply unpleasant. The mind has both instinctual and learning abilities and horrifying or disgusting experiences can impact the mind for the long term. In soldiers, and now more frequently in others having experienced "trauma," this is called PTSD, or Post Traumatic Stress Disorder. (Though my son, Mastin Kipp, thinks the word "disorder" should be replaced with "Response" since PTSD/R is mostly related to the biology of the Vagus nerve. For more, Google Vagal Nerve Theory.)

I put trauma in quotes because we don't all have the same definition for it. I call trauma a deeply distressing or disturbing experience; so, at least you now know where I'm coming from. We each define (or discover), for ourselves what is "distressing" or "disturbing." It's part cultural, part biological, and partly learned on the spot, but it's mostly individual. What may be traumatic for you may not be so for me, and *vice versa*.

The point is that if a trauma occurred, then we have to learn to cope with it, perhaps even cure it, if possible. Not all do, or can. In war, you may not even know that a trauma occurred until later; other times you know right when it happens. And trauma may also become chronic. Stephen King wrote, "The truth is that monsters are real, and ghosts are real, too. They live inside us, and sometimes they win."

So, getting back to "gross." The Vietnam War taught me that the gross things in life are related to the after-effects of human activity, and ignorance. A head, neatly severed and lying on its side in the grass is gross. Inspecting a wounded child and placing your finger in his damaged ear and seeing your finger come out where his eye should be is gross. Cleaning up after a mass causality situation, only to find a brain hemisphere left behind is gross. Treating a live, wounded woman and picking her up, only to have her macheted skull cap slide off and have her brains slide out is gross. Taking a 50-pound man rescued from an underground NVA hospital and finding out he was kept as a human blood bank for two years in their tunnel bunker is gross. Feverishly giving blood to a GI who had injected himself with peanut butter oil to get high is gross. Administering mouth-to-mouth resuscitation to a GI, only to have his last living act be to vomit into your mouth is gross. Flying into a Green Beret camp and not being able to land without landing on a body is gross. Treating an old Vietnamese man who walked by a US Army camp at dusk and was shot in a game of target practice is gross.

These are some of the traumas I have experienced that I now find myself able to mention, though not talk about in detail. There are others I still can't go back to, not yet. There were a lot of traumas experienced in the War by people on both sides, and those caught in the middle. It really burns me the wrong way when I see a panhandling Vietnam Vet being ignored, or worse, being abused by others. They never walked in his shoes. They can't even imagine it.

But I can talk about the mental processes I went through during a Dustoff mission. The pre-pickup phase is pretty standard: I run to the chopper and if I am there before the pilot, I unhook the rotorblade, then check my medic bag and supplies to make sure, again, I'll have what I'll need. The pilot will enter the cockpit and yell, "Clear?!" and Tom and I each on our side of the chopper with the engine view panel pushed open each yell, "Clear!" The pilot starts the turbine engine and I watch the engine for fuel and oil leaks and anything out of the ordinary. If I see something, I tell the pilot to stop; if I don't then I remain observant of the turbine until we have reached a good rotor RPM. I then get into my side (left) of the chopper, look around for anything the pilot needs to know and if okay I say, "Clear left!" Tom says, "Clear right!" and we take off.

I loved take offs. Sitting there at the open door, inches from falling out, and watching people until they become ants and all the details of the ground blend into a mosaic quiltwork of open ground, forests, rice paddies bounded by lines which I knew to be roads. The air got better too. It was no longer hot and stuffy, it was cooler with a stiff breeze back where I sat, looking backwards, checking for any nearby aircraft on the left rear that the pilot may need to know about. I felt like I owned the world. The AC and pilot would chatter back and forth about the flight path to the LZ. If it was a routine flight, the AC might even turn on the Armed Forces Radio for a while.

"We need to go north five clicks before turning west to avoid artillery coming from that firebase over there." We would look and see puffs of smoke as the artillery was launched at the unknown enemy. This also told me it could be a hot LZ with enemy still nearby. "Check your weapon!" I'd check my CAR-15 to see if it was ready. (My Colt Automatic Rifle was a Commando, like an M-16, with an ultra-short barrel so I could swing it around easily inside the chopper from one side to the other). Clip full and reset. Locked and loaded. Check. A few minutes later the AC would contact the LZ radio operator to ask for an update. The RTO responded, "Dustoff, we have four WIAs (Wounded in Action]) and one KIA (Killed in Action), over." The AC asks for the nature of the wounds: "Dustoff, three gunshot wounds and one burn victim, over." The AC looks at me to see if I have enough information and I ask for them to load the most wounded patient first, which the AC relays to the ground. "Roger that," they respond.

We are now close to the LZ but have not pinpointed it yet. I can see artillery shells exploding in an area and I start looking for colored smoke nearby. The AC tells the radio operator to "Pop smoke." He responds "Roger." Tom, the AC, and I crane our necks looking for colored smoke. Tom yells, "Got it, at two o'clock, low." The copilot confirms he sees it and the AC asks the radio operator if the smoke is green. Once confirmed the AC asks if there was a preferred line of approach. "Recommend approach from the north, over."

The ground is undulating wooded hills with a large stream. The smoke is near the stream and the artillery fire is landing on the other side of the stream. We can now see that the open area where the smoke is, is actually just an area with some cut down or blown trees. There will be no solid ground to land on, we'll be at a hover while loading. The pilot approaches the LZ by coming down to treetop level about a half mile north of the site and we approach the site, slowing.

At tree top level we are less visible to snipers. The open area becomes visible and the pilot scans the site to determine how and where to lower the chopper. As we come in, Tom and I switch our attention to the chopper and how close the blades, tail rotor and skids are to obstacles. We relay information to the pilot and he adjusts the chopper while bringing us lower. Tom says, "Stop. Tail can't go any farther here. Need to rotate tail to the left," which is my cue to check the area where the tail might rotate in my direction.

I say, "Tail clear to come 90 degrees left." The pilot, at a hover, rotates the tail left 90 degrees. I look down and say, "You are clear on the left to descend, Tom?"

Tom replies, "Looks like we're good to come down." The pilot drops us down, and we give him numbers to indicate how many feet he needs to come down.

Something like, "Twenty feet to go on the left side, rotor and tail clear."

Tom then responds and then the pilot brings us down. Tom yells, "One foot," then there is a bump and he adds, "Hold!" Then we offload four litters then begin to load on the patients.

Because we are up in the fallen trees, everyone's footing on the ground is a bit iffy. They load the first patient on, which should be the most critically wounded, and we move him into the area just behind the pilot and AC chairs. The next litter is loaded and Tom and I lift it to the highest position on the litter rack. We do the same with the third litter. Gunfire opens up on the ground. We ignore it and take on the fourth litter, moving it into the litter rack under the other two. Then, the body bag containing the KIA is loaded and placed in the rear seat. Hauling KIAs is just as cumbersome as hauling wounded. If we hadn't been in a hot LZ, we would have asked them to have somebody else pick up the KIA. But there was no time. After the KIA was loaded, I yell at the GI helping the loading and ask if there are any more wounded. He shakes his head no. I tell the pilot, "We're done here."

We then need to lift our chopper, still surrounded by upright trees, out of the hole they cut for us. As we come up we give directions and advice to the pilot, who expertly lifts us out of the trees and back into open air. He reverses his course and takes us back the way we came, at low level and gaining speed for half a mile, then we start gaining altitude. The AC advises about strafing aircraft paths and the co-pilot adjusts his course to avoid them.

Once we are out of gunshot range, I lower my CAR 15 and take a look at my first patient. Tom, my crew chief, follows my lead and looks after the others. I know he will tell me if there is something that needs my immediate attention. I check breathing, bleeding, shock, and the need for blood volume expanders. This guy needed an IV. With Tom's help I am finally able to find a vein on his right arm and gave him a bottle of Ringer's. *Damn.*

Three gunshot wounds have been bandaged. I check the entry and exit holes of each wound; usually the exit hole is three or more times bigger than the entry wound. I take stock— one shoulder wound, one to the far-left side of the chest. I stop to look for a sucking chest wound to indicate a collapsed lung. Finding one, I place a Vaseline saturated piece of bandage to cover and seal it on both sides to keep it airtight. The third wound is to the left leg, right through the knee.

In each case, I remove the field-battle dressings and visually inspect the wounds. With the knee I first had to use my scissors to cut his clothing to give me a better view, then I removed the dressing. I found a fair amount of bleeding, too much to make me happy, so I grabbed my clamps and clamped three vessels. Bleeding stopped. Good. I put the old dressing back on and wrap it with gauze tape just to hold everything in place. I have to tape the clamps in place.

Three more to go. I look the others over and we had one head wound, a superficial wound that scraped the skull but nothing broken; one gunshot to the arm, again bleeding contained; and the burn patient. This guy was conscious with willie peter (white phosphorous) burns on his arm and face. I put Vaseline over these to keep out any oxygen and ask him how he feels. He says they don't hurt anymore but his butt hurts. I take a look and see a bullet grazed his butt. I patch it and tell him and he said it must have happened after he fell down. "My DI always told me to keep my big ass butt down!" he says, grinning.

I gave the AC a report on our wounded and requested the hospital provide me with three clamps. The AC relayed that information to the hospital. When we landed, eight medics were there to help unload the wounded. They gave us four litters and three clamps to replace the ones I used. Sometimes they don't give you the clamps and not having enough when you need them is a bitch. You can never have too many clamps.

When we get back, Tom checks out the chopper for any damage or need for repairs. He enters things into his log book. I clean out the chopper of all the blood, bandages, and other debris, such as that tree branch over in the corner, then take stock of my supplies. I place the three clamps where they are handy, and head for the hospital to pick up some additional rolls of gauze and tape.

An hour after we land, Tom and I are back in the RTO trying to figure out where we were in our game of cribbage.

44 MY VIETNAMESE BARBER AT DAU TIENG USED A STRAIGHT RAZOR

AS I SAID, WE ALSO KEPT ONE FIRST Up chopper at Dau Tieng. In this area we mainly covered the 25th Infantry Division and sometimes the 199th Light Infantry Brigade. Unlike being at the main base at Lai Khe, where we had four crews ready, at Dau Tieng we only had one chopper. During my time there, I was the only Dustoff medic on site so I was always, 24-7, ready to go. That meant I never went very far from the RTO shack. Sometimes during our three-day stint we would get no calls, other times we could easily use up our 25 hours of flight time before the expected replacement date.

Someone once said, "War is days of boredom punctuated by moments of terror." That's pretty close. One day at Dau Tieng my co-pilot came back and said he just got a haircut and a shave from a barbershop about 30 yards away. I hadn't ever wandered that far and decided I wanted to go, and off I went. This guy was great. His name was Wu. Excellent and quick haircut, and a real shave, with hot towels, abundant, creamy shaving cream, and a great aftershave that cooled in the hot Vietnamese weather. He always made a great deal about sharpening the straight razor on his strop. *Whack...whack...whack.* Then he'd put his thumb on the blade to test its sharpness. That blade was so smooth. It never tugged, never pulled, it just sliced through my beard like I was rubbing my finger across my face and throat. I had become used to shaving with cold water or not using any water at all, a dry shave. If it's humid enough it's not so bad. But this shave...I was hooked, and thereafter always looked forward to getting my haircut and a shave from Wu every couple of weeks.

One night we got a call. Three gunshot wounds; unsecured LZ. We called in a Cobra gunship and went to pick them up. We came in and there were now five wounded. All gunshot wounds. One of them was a VC POW. We loaded the litters onto the chopper and I went through each patient as they were loaded to ascertain who needed treatment first. I then cleared the left side of the chopper and we took off. There were two American GIs with serious bleeding. I checked their other side for exit wounds, cleared their airways, stopped their bleeding, then gave them Ringer's IV solutions as a blood volume expander. I then went to the VC POW. His face was covered in blood. He had a bloody, but non-life-threatening wound on the forehead, and a gunshot wound to the leg. I went through my routine, including an IV, then got out my hydrogen peroxide and started to clean his face. Once his face became clear, I recognized him. It was the barber, Wu! I said hello, then went to the other two GIs.

Later that night, after we were safely back in the RTO shack, we got a call that the POW we'd brought in was the VC Colonel for the unit the US infantry were battling. I spent all that night trying to count all the times a VC Colonel had a straight razor at my throat. My count was fourteen.

45 SOMETIMES, THERE'S NOTHING YOU CAN DO

A CALL CAME IN TO THE RTO AT Lai Khe to pick up some Vietnamese civilians who had been wounded by the VC. On our flight out, the AC tried to determine the nature of the wounds, but the call had been relayed secondhand from some South Vietnamese Army soldiers who spoke little English. We came in, and I recall while we positioned the chopper seeing a few native houses, and a small crowd of civilians near a small child. We landed and I ran over to the crowd, and they pointed me to the child.

The mother was holding the child's shoulders and crying her heart out. I moved in and examined the child. My first glance showed a head wound. I checked the airway and looked for other wounds. Finding none I then examined the head wound carefully. There was a cut line that went all the way across the forehead where the head hair meets. I brushed the child's hair, to get a clear look at the wound, and all of a sudden, the top of the head slid off and part of the child's brains slid out onto the ground. The child had been macheted at the top of the head.

I looked at the mother, who was bawling in disbelief. I grabbed her shoulders, stood her up, and looked her straight in the eyes. Then I shook my head. I hugged her, and then went back to the chopper and we left. Sometimes, there's just nothing you can do.

46 WHEN 30 = 49

I TOOK MY FIRST 30-DAY LEAVE IN NOVEMBER 1968. I'd been there over a year by then—14 months. I chose to go home. I flew first to San Francisco. When we landed, I kissed the ground. I recall being very worried that a major earthquake would happen while I was at the airport. When our flight direct to Philadelphia took off, I breathed a sigh of relief and thought, *Okay earthquake, you can happen now.* I arrived just before Thanksgiving.

My Dad met me at the airport. I saw him looking at me and, as usual, I couldn't read his face. As we approached he put his hand out to shake, but I just grabbed and hugged him. It was like hugging a mannequin. He didn't hug back. Mom told me years later after he died that he once said, "Hugging is what women do."

At home it was the usual catch up, with me being very careful not to let them know I was in any danger. Unlike my stoic Dad, my mom was very transparent about her worries. "The war," I said, "is pretty much over," waving with one arm indicating somewhere other than where I was in Vietnam. That seemed to put Mom at ease.

I visited with my folks at home for about a week, but I also wanted to catch up with my old high school friends. The Kathy thing was over, though I hadn't yet figured out that was a good thing. All the girls I knew back home were paired up. After a week of catching up, I started thinking of Chewy in Kansas. Next thing I knew I was on a flight to Kansas City (the Army would reimburse all my travel expenses while on leave). By the time I arrived at my old university, Thanksgiving break was over and all the students had returned, including Chewy. We laughed, loved, and cried. I stayed a week then headed back to Wilmington and I hung out with some of the guys I grew up with. It was now the second week in December, and I had to return to 'Nam on the 21st. I thought, *Hell, leave for 'Nam four days before*

Christmas? I can't do that to Mom. When I told Mom I was staying a little longer and would be there for Christmas, she cried with joy.

I was completely ignorant of the riot that had taken place in our city, Wilmington, Delaware, in the spring after the assassination of Dr. Martin Luther King. The governor had called out the National Guard and they were still patrolling when I returned home in the late fall.

I did see a few military trucks as I moved about but that's all I had seen for over a year, so by comparison there were damn few of them and not noticeable to me.

Back at home on Christmas Eve, I took a possible girlfriend, Linda (a friend of Kathy's), to the candlelight service at her church, which was Episcopalian. I knew nothing about these "other" Christians and felt like I was entering possible enemy territory. With religion you never know. Linda had asked me to wear my Army dress uniform so I did.

We were waiting for others to arrive, when a hippie came in and sat next to me in the pew. After getting himself situated, he looked at me, got up and left. It was only then that Linda, in whispers, told me about the National Guard situation. In my mind I spoke to the hippie and said: "Okay, I'm going to forgive you, but before I do, fuck you. Now I forgive you."

I went to my folk's church, Concord Presbyterian Church, a few times while I was back, too. I recall one time I met one of my parents' friends, and older English woman who had married a GI and moved back to the States with him after WWII. We hadn't seen each other in quite a while, and she asked me where I had been. I said, "I've been in the war." She looked at me quizzically, and said, "What war?" It was then I realized the separateness I have felt ever since with "civilians." I had seen a lot of terrible things done to people, including women and children, did the best I could to keep them from dying, living those memories in my dreams— memories and thoughts that this woman, and all the other civilians I would meet hereafter, could never imagine, let alone comprehend. I realized I was apart from "the civilians" and that barrier has never come down. It pops right up every time I hear things that are contrary to the Constitution, a document every soldier is sworn to protect and defend.

The week of Christmas was like homecoming again. Everyone was back from college and it was a great reunion. On the 28th I thought, *Damn, New Year's is in a few days. I'll leave after the 1st.* That's what I did. I hadn't counted up the days I was late in returning, but I began to think maybe it was too much.

I went to Fort Dix on the 3rd and flew out via Anchorage on the 4th, which was still the 3rd in Vietnam. When I got to Ton Son Nhut airbase I was able to raise Lai Khe Dustoff on the radio and told them I was here. A few hours later, Maj. Smith f lew down with my Crew Chief and a co-pilot. I was surprised to see my Crew Chief in the co-pilot's seat.

After our hellos, Maj. Smith said he let Tom fly the chopper down and would I like to fly her back to Lai Khe? "Yes!" I said. So I got in the co-pilot's seat (on the right), Tom slid my side armor forward and shut my door. Maj. Smith flew the chopper away from the airbase and once we got altitude he started prepping me on "how to think about flying." Basically, there is the "stick," located between my legs, used to tilt the rotor blade and give you forward, sideways, or backward motion; there is the "collective," an emergency brake-like pull rod to my left, used to provide positive or negative lift on the rotorblades; and the foot pedals, used to keep the anti- torque tail rotor in the desired position. After ten minutes he let me grab the stick. "The stick is in the same orientation and tilt as the rotor shaft," he said. "What the stick does, the rotor shaft does." With my hand on the stick he jostled the stick and I felt the stick slightly move and the chopper respond as well.

"Notice I did not move the stick much," he said. "Now we need the stick placed slightly forward to give us the forward motion. Now, see that cloud over there?" I saw it. He said, "Okay, now, while you are holding the stick, just *think* about heading that way." I did, and we started to head that way. "So you see, the controls are very sensitive. You need to become one with the machine. 'Feel' the tail rotor, make it a part of your body. 'Feel' the skids and make them your legs. For now, just take the stick and get us to Lai Khe." He took his hands off the stick and let me fly it. Wow, it was great, and a bit overwhelming.

After another ten minutes I was calmed down and Maj. Smith told me to switch the helmet mike channel to 2. I did, and then realized I was on the channel where the AC and co- pilot could talk without the crew in the back hearing. Then he said to me, "Ya know, you're AWOL, over 10 days AWOL." I didn't say a thing, but the chopper shuddered a bit and changed direction.

After a minute I said, "I'm sorry sir, it was just too close to Christmas, and then New Year's," I said. I struggled to think in the direction the chopper had to go.

I looked at Maj. Smith. He looked at me and said, "Well, if you promise not to do it again, I'll let it pass."

All my tension melted away. Then I felt like an asshole for being so selfish and leaving my team members one man short for so long. I hadn't even thought about *that*. I then apologized to him and told him it was a major mistake in my judgment. I said, "Thank you for letting me learn from my mistake."

When we approached Lai Khe, Maj. Smith took over and we landed without incident. I was really happy to see everyone and told everyone to come to my hooch ASAP. As people arrived, I unpacked my duffle bag. People realized that half the bag was filled with "travel wrapped" submarine sandwiches from the Arden Sub Shop near Wilmington. They were loaded up: meats, cheese, pickles, onion, banana peppers, olive oil, lettuce, tomatoes, and black pepper on a 12" hard roll. By this time they were three days old, but in forty-five minutes they were all gone. For me, three-day-old subs are just perfect—if they came from the Arden Sub Shop.

I went into the RTO to get my medic pack I had placed on the wall before I left. I checked all the supplies and discovered that all my morphine syrettes were gone. It was then I realized we had a drug problem in the unit. We had all smoked pot, but opium usage was a different animal and unknown to me until then. As I learned later, hallucinogenic drugs and pot rarely resulted in theft, unlike the narcotic drugs like opium and cocaine that became more common much later. It was January 1969. The pot smoking in 'Nam began once the hippies started getting drafted, trained, and sent over in mid-1968.

The attitude of the soldiers I met daily changed. Before, it was, "Well, I didn't want to come but my country asked me to go, so I did." After the hippies started to arrive, that attitude diminished and was replaced by one of easily aroused hostility and anger at being there.

In disagreement over illegalities, one of the quick replies was, "What are they gonna do, send me to 'Nam?"

47 LISTENING TO MUSIC

MUSIC IN NAM WAS HARD TO COME BY. We had small AM radios that received the local Armed Forces Radio broadcasts, and every morning there was this guy, at 6 AM, on the radio saying, "GOOOOOOOOOOOOOOOOOOOOD MOOOOORRRRRRRNNNNNIG VEEEEEEEEEE-ET-NAMMM!" I hated it. In Vung Tau I bought a tape recorder—a huge, cumbersome device that weighed about 25 pounds. I bought large reels of taped music, mostly Lou Rawles, because that's what was available in the Px for my player. At Lai Khe one of the crew chiefs had a record player and speakers. They were set up down in the Bolt Hole (bunker) which had been made pretty cozy with blankets, electric posters, and a blue lightbulb. The player had been stolen when I was at the 36th and laid up in the hospital for ten days with pneumonia and I never did recover it.

I remember the day Casper got *Sgt. Pepper's Lonely Hearts Club Band* by the Beatles in the mail. We smoked pot, drank beer, and listened to the album. Wow. It was cool. By the end of the album we were relaxed and just absorbing the music. We found the song "Being for the Benefit of Mr. Kite!" really interesting. It evoked a spookiness that was enhanced by the fact that we were in a bunker and there were people just outside the nearby perimeter who wanted us dead. Someone turned the volume up high and ran outside and hid behind the rubber trees. The five of us all followed, then he pranced to the next tree to the beat of the music, and so on. We all laughed and followed. That song seemed spooky, so being in the dark, in a dangerous place, beer in hand, just seemed right. At the time it was great. But you had to be there.

Until I got to Long Binh in 1969, I had never seen pot except as rolled joints offered by someone else. Down in Long Binh, I was asked if I wanted to "go in on" a Ritz tin filled with Cambodian Red. "How much?" I asked, and I was told $5. "Each?"

"No," was the reply. "Five dollars for the whole tin." I then realized that the pot coming in to us was mostly coming from Cambodia. I knew that poppies were grown in the Golden Triangle, and I had heard the warlords there needed to get their "product" to market. I thought about those STOL (Short Take Off and Landing) aircraft with "Air America" I had seen so often coming in and out of Cambodia up near Song Be, and wondered.

48 A HUMAN BLOOD BANK, VC STYLE

I WAS SITTING IN THE RTO SHACK AT Dau Tieng doing a crossword puzzle when a call came in to medivac some Vietnamese civilians who had been VC prisoners near Cu Chi. On our flight over we were told that none of them were injured but they needed to go to a hospital. There were three to pick up.

We came into the LZ, landed, and the 25th Infantry guys ran over to our chopper with the litters. As we loaded them, I thought I was looking at skeletons or the dead. I asked the Lieutenant who helped bring them over if they were alive and the guy said, "Yes, we pulled them out of a VC tunnel. It was a VC hospital and they were using these guys as blood banks."

That was a new one. We finished loading them and took off. They all had saline IVs and were properly tagged—something rare. The only bandages they had were on their left arms. It looked as if there had been some sort of permanent needle attachment so they could just spigot out the needed blood. There were no infections apparent either. But these people . . . I was never able to adequately describe how they looked until I saw the *Band of Brothers* episode where they liberated a concentration camp. That is exactly how they looked. Sunken cheeks, hollow eyes, no glimmer in the eyeballs, skin shrunken down to the bone. One had lost a lot of hair. They didn't speak a word.

After I left Vietnam, this was one of my episodes that kept coming back to me. I asked, *How could they do this?* I could never forgive them. It wasn't until 49 years later, when I returned to Vietnam and had a three-hour discussion with an old Buddhist monk about forgiveness that I was able to put it to rest. He said, "Even if you can't forgive, speak towards Love." After fifty years, that was all I needed to hear.

49 LANDING WITHOUT A TAIL ROTOR

RANDY "ROTORBLADES" RADIGAN WAS AC AND WO QUAIL (aka "Feather") was our pilot on a 3-day stint at Quan Loi, up near the "Fish Hook" and the Cambodian border. We got a call to come and pick up a wounded fellah from the Big Red One, AKA the 1st Infantry Division. We located the site only because they had cut down a tree or two. We could see them down in the trees. Randy came in slowly and hovered, then went down ever so slowly. We didn't have a hoist so we needed to get down and pull the wounded up.

Tom Cash, my crew chief called out to Randy, "Okay, move the tail to the right about 90 degrees." The chopper rotated 90 degrees left, then he said, "Okay, come on down a bit . . . okay, hold! That's as far as you can go."

I said, "No, you can come left about 70 degrees." He came left 90 degrees and into a tree. It felt like slow motion as the rear rotor chewed its way through a large branch. Then, suddenly, we spun around twice and up we went, still spinning round and round. We tilted and started moving in one direction, still spinning. Eventually the spin stopped, and we were flying, albeit awkwardly. Rather than the chopper nose being pointed in the direction of flight, it was pointed about 20 degrees off to the right of the direction we were flying. So long as we had an airspeed of about 70 knots the chopper would "streamline," meaning it would tend to point in the direction of f light, just by the air pressure flowing around the craft like a weathervane. Normally the tail rotor would counteract the spin of the blade (which wants to turn the whole chopper in the opposite direction of spin, hence the tail rotor as the solution).

We called Quon Loi Tower and requested emergency landing. They granted it immediately. We made a "running landing" using the skids. We came in and hit the PSP (perforated steel plating used to "pave" a runway in a hurry) at 70 knots. As we coasted to a stop (which seemed to take forever) Tom and I climbed out onto the skids and opened the AC's and co-pilot's doors and pulled back the pilot protector shields, so they could make a quick exit once we stopped. It was then I looked down and saw the PSP (steel-plated runway), only 3 inches away from my boots, streaming past. Eventually we came to a halt and shut down. We did not complete our mission.

50 TAKING FIRE

ON DAYS AND NIGHTS OF CONTINUAL FIGHTING, WE got few chances to rest. We would pick up wounded until we ran low on fuel, then go refuel, then go out and pick up some more. Our job ended pretty much about three hours after whenever the fighting stopped. When we did return home, my crew chief and I went about our usual routine cleaning and checking out the chopper and updating the log book. Occasionally we would end up with some of the gear that belonged to one of the patients. It would be impossible to know which patient the gear belonged to, so it was usually appropriated by us or used in the ante at the next poker game.

I'd been issued an M-16, but I ended up with a CAR-15 (xM-177) Commando rifle that had a shorter barrel than the M-16, which was great when maneuvering it inside a helicopter. It used the same ammo as the M-16, but I never trusted my M-16. The first time I used my issued M-16, it jammed after getting off two shots. There I was, firing down at the enemy who were firing up at us and I get two rounds off and it jams. Damn! They kept shooting until we got out of range, and I was left there wondering what the fuck was wrong with my fucking rifle. No one got hit that time, but Tom was unhappy about the bullet holes in *The Judge* and the leaking hydraulic line. I tested my CAR-15 out at the perimeter of our base. It worked fine and later it never let me down.

We took fire a lot when approaching, loading, or departing LZs. We called these hot LZs. There's nothing much to say, we did our job of loading patients, fired back on arrival and departure when necessary, took care of the wounded once out of range, and went on.

Sometimes we got shot ourselves. I was never hit by a bullet, but my fatigues got bullet holes in them, so they were close. Sometimes passengers got hit. Taking fire made for more work for the Crew Chief, for sure. He had to go over every inch of the chopper after we took fire. Every inch. An AK-47 bullet hole is not large—the entry hole is about 7.62 mm or about 0.3 inches wide. There are lots of spaces in a Dustoff where a bullet can pass right through and not damage anything critical. There are other places where a single hit can down the chopper, especially in the hydraulics. Then there are other hits that should have downed the chopper but didn't because of exceptional piloting abilities of the AC or co-pilot. The Crew Chief has to look for the bullet holes, find them, repair them, then brag about them later at the Clubhouse, which was often visited by the hospital staff.

The pilots were fairly protected from bullets, except from the front or lower front. The seat had armor, and there were the side protectors we slid into place after they seated themselves. But the head was always exposed, and we still had pilots getting shot. Their lower legs were completely exposed.

Once Lt. Dan Weaver (Dustoff 45) got hit in the leg and the crew chief, Casper, got shrapnel when they had to do a low-level departure from a hot LZ due to the jets making bomb runs. They low-levelled right over an enemy squad and were nailed by AK47 fire. Two of the patients were killed. For us in the back, we wore bullet protector vests, and sat on bullet proof armor plate squares about as big as your butt that could slide around the floor. One crew chief painted a yellow stripe down the back of his vest. When asked "why?" he replied, "If they know I'm a chicken maybe they'll shoot someone else." Everybody had their own way of coping.

Our helmets were standard, olive drab, flight helmets with no ballistic protection that I know of. Co-pilots often painted their helmets with unique designs, some quite intricate. ACs often ditched their customized helmets once they made AC and used an unadorned one.

Remember, we were all only about 19 years old but the new ACs wanted to be accepted by their higher ups.

51 MIGHTY TERMITES

I DID AS MUCH BOTANIZING AS I COULD at Lai Khe. Everything was new, so there was a lot to take in. My mom sent me vegetable seeds to grow and the locals wanted everything I grew, except the watermelon. Their melons were better.

One of the things I noticed in my botanizing was a termite mound back behind our area near where we burned our shit. Burning shit was the only safe way to dispose of it. In fact, every day a half million GI turds got burned in Vietnam. Anywhere the US was, there was the smell of burning shit. All the EMs burned shit at least once, and many did so many times. We called it our "primary MOS" (Military Occupational Specialty). Every time I burned shit I stared at that termite mound. I couldn't see over it, so it was at least six feet high. I knew termites were social animals, and that they had a caste system with a queen, many workers, and soldier termites as well, with really big jaws.

We were located right next to the perimeter. We were a rubber plantation in the middle of a jungle. The generals didn't like that jungle up so close, so they started knocking trees down to provide some lines of fire for defense. Some engineers came to Lai Khe in a pack. Eventually, the engineers brought in some Rome plows— armored, specially modified bulldozers with a large blade for clearing large trees. The whole thing weighed about 25 tons. I was fascinated, in a morbid sort of way, to see ten Rome Plows, one after the other, lined up to clear the forest. No trees in our neck of the woods could stop these suckers.

In a couple of weeks, our side of the perimeter was cleared back a full mile. No more trees for the VC to hide behind. We now had really good, interlocking lines of fire from our perimeter.

Over the course of the next few months I noticed that out beyond the perimeter, new termite mounds started appearing. Just like the one I contemplated while burning shit. I was amazed at how many of them there were. Literally hundreds of them.

My curiosity became so aroused that I went in search of a shovel. I decided to disassemble the one in our back yard to see what it was like inside. I got one of our shovels and went to spade out a part of the mound. Clang. My shovel did not even put a dent in it. I was surprised; this thing was hard!

With my curiosity really roused, I went in search of a pickaxe. Pleased that I had found one, I approached the mound with the anticipation that I was now going to have my way with it. Like a golfer, I addressed the mound. I placed my feet firmly down, grasped the pickaxe with both hands, lifted it up over my head, and swung down as hard as I could. Two things happened simultaneously. First the pickaxe came to a complete stop. Then, what I felt, first in my hands then all the way up my arms, was the full energy of the swing being sent from the point of contact, up the handle, and into me. It was like an electric shock and it knocked me down.

Once I got my wits, I looked at where I hit the mound and could not find the point of contact. I was stunned, literally and intellectually. I knew termites used their saliva and mixed it with the soil to make their mounds. But I had no idea the end product was so hard. I searched the mound for any exits, knowing termites don't like to be in exposed to low-humidity air. I found one with a soldier termite, jaws wide open, at the entrance. *That* would be my next target. I dug at it with the point of the pickaxe to no avail.

I thought a spike and a hammer might work. Nope. Maybe a spike and a sledge. Finally, I managed to get a chip knocked out—small, about two inches around. Soldier termites swarmed out all over the place, crawling everywhere, and it soon became a place I did not want to be. I came back later and found a new scar where I had done my minor surgery on the mound. I was impressed.

Weeks later I went to the perimeter and I saw the mounds out there had grown even more. They were now big enough for Charlie to hide behind and crawl all the way up to our perimeter. I really became impressed with the concept of " unintended consequences."

52 LOST IN A FOG

WHILE AT QUAN LOI WE GOT A CALL to pick up a gunshot wound up near the border, in the mountains. As we headed toward our target, the clouds moved in. We were in fog. We had a new co-pilot who had been with us a couple of weeks. Dustoff 41, Randy "Rotorblades" Radigan, was our AC. The co-pilot was flying while the AC was trying to raise the target on the radio.

Nothing. We were now flying by instruments. Based on our direction and flying time, with the assumption made of our ground speed, we approached what we thought was the target area. The AC tried again on the radio: nothing.

After five minutes he began using alternative radio frequencies. On each frequency he repeated, "Delta Tango Foxtrot, this is Dustoff 41, do you read?" over and over. Nothing. Then, on one channel we heard a double click. That usually meant that the target was in a compromised position and could not speak. The AC repeated the message, and again, there was a double click. The AC said, "We read, will wait, over." Double click.

After another five minutes the radio crackled, and in a whispering voice the person on the other end said, "Dustoff 41, please identify."

Our AC said, "Delta Tango Foxtrot, this is Dustoff 41, we are here to pick up your gunshot wound, over."

The voice said, "What is your location, over."

"Delta Tango Foxtrot, we are at, or near, Yankee Uniform three zero zero three zero five, over."

There was a pause, then, "Dustoff 41, say again?" The AC repeated the coordinates. "Dustoff 41, what's your latitude?" said the voice.

"Delta Tango Foxtrot, we are between North Latitude 11 and 12, over."

There was at least a minute's pause, then the voice came back. "Dustoff 41, be advised, we are north of 38, over. This communication is terminated. Please get off this restricted frequency, over."

Everybody in the chopper looked at everybody else. "That guy was in Korea!" yelled Randy. Almost 2,000 miles away! The weather had to be just right for that kind of "line of sight" communication to bounce around. The co-pilot reminded us all that we had been in the air 65 minutes, so we now had less than two hours of fuel left. Randy told us we were going to complete this mission. "There's somebody out there that needs us," he said on the mic.

We had been in the fog about forty minutes. We had been on station about 25 minutes.

Being "on station" meant that we were widely circling our presumed target area. The AC tried all the radio frequencies, and there were no responses on any of them. He then began calling Quan Loi RTO. No response. We could not raise anyone on any frequency. Then Randy said, "I think the radio is out."

My Crew Chief, Tom Cash, said, "Everything checked out on the last inspection with avionics, which was only six [flying] hours ago." We flew for another few minutes while Randy and the co-pilot talked amongst themselves.

All I had to do was either chat with Tom or look out at the fog. So I did both. One time Tom was talking to me while I was looking at him. I looked up to check my bottle of Ringer's solution hanging from a hook on the ceiling when I realized the bottle was lying flat against the ceiling. I pointed that out to Tom and he freaked out, got on the intercom with the pilots, and told them we were in a dive. They looked back, saw the bottle, then the AC took over and seemingly levelled us out. The copilot tapped on the altimeter and it suddenly shifted from 2,500 feet elevation to 920 feet elevation. "It was stuck!" said the co-pilot. At that point the AC, Randy, said, "I've lost all confidence in these instruments. The radio, the altimeter, and the artificial horizon indicator all failed. I am switching to VFR and taking the controls. Cap," he said to the co-pilot, "Keep an eye on that IV bottle."

We began to climb. It had felt like we were flying level and none of us had a sense that we were in a spiraling dive. Randy called it a gyroscopic dive and said it had something to do with the physics of blade rotation and the geometry of our downward spiral path. We were all a bit pale now.

The mission was over; it was now a matter of keeping us flying and getting home. During the episode we also realized that we had lost any sense of direction. Randy decided to rely on the compass and he turned us southwest. The co-pilot had a compass on his watch and checked it, confirming that we were heading southwest. For the rest of the flight that Ringer's bottle was our artificial horizon indicator. The co-pilot again tried the radio. No luck.

After another hour Randy said he thought it would be okay to come down a bit, since we should now be out of the mountains. He asked Tom and I to keep an eye out for anything visible below us. At regular intervals the co-pilot tapped the altimeter to see if it would readjust again. We were at 1,500 feet when the 20-minute warning light came on. Still just fog. I asked Tom, "What's a 20-minute warning light?" and he told me that that was how much flying time we had before we ran out of fuel.

"Oh," I said, as I tried to let that sink in.

The radio was tried again, still no contact with anyone. We could get Armed Forces Radio though, which was curious, so we listened to that. I think Randy wanted that playing just to help keep us calm, though I wasn't worried, just alert and wondering. Randy said he was coming down some more, and would continue a slow decent until "we either land or hit something." He also slowed his guessed air speed.

Later during that twenty minutes I spied a light and alerted the pilots. Randy came around to put it in his view and we lost it. He stopped his decline and we took a leisurely turn. Suddenly he saw a helicopter on the ground, parked. Randy turned on our landing lights and looked around. Right next to the chopper on the ground was an empty revetment. He moved our chopper over to it and slowly edged his way into it. Suddenly, the engine stopped. We did a hovering autorotation onto the ground. Randy said we were four feet off the ground when we ran out of fuel.

When I got out, I could just barely see the other chopper in the revetment next to ours through the thick fog. The base lights were on, but I could only see one, with a faint orange glow behind that one. I could tell from the insignia on the chopper next to us that we were at a 1st Cavalry base. It turned out to be **Phước Vinh**, about 35 clicks from where we had tried to go— just under 22 miles.

The next morning the fog cleared and we refueled and flew to Lai Khe via VFR and had the avionics given a thorough going over. Randy consulted a map and found that the lowest elevation he could find in the area where we thought we were when we took that dive to 920 feet was 890 feet. He concluded that we must have dived between the mountains into a valley. "That IV bottle saved our lives," he said.

53 CREWING ON A HUEY

CREWING ON A HUEY WAS ABSOLUTELY FABULOUS. EVERYONE knew their tasks and the four of us worked as a team. On occasion someone would rotate into the unit and not work out.

Not work out. I've thought about that and I want to try and explain what that means.

Where to begin? You want the people you are working with to be looking out for you.

You want them to cover your back, just like you'll cover theirs. FNGs to the unit needed to prove that before they were accepted. It boils down to trust. "Can I trust this FNG to watch my back while I'm paying attention to doing my job, or do I have to divide my attention between watching my back and doing my job?"

As Dustoff people we took pride in the job we did. Our Motto came from Dustoff pilot Maj. Charles Kelly, who earned the Medal of Honor while rescuing wounded in 1964. He said, "No compromise. No rationalization. No hesitation. Fly the mission. Now!" We instinctively knew our mission posed some risks, but I never knew until after the war when some number cruncher examined all the mission reports that the life expectancy of a Dustoff crew in a hot LZ was 30 seconds. Dustoff choppers in Vietnam were 3.3 times more likely to get shot down than any other form of helicopter mission.[4] Everyone needed to be sharp, paying attention, and looking out for everyone else. We wanted that from our replacements too.

We had a medic come into the unit that always wore his prescription sunglasses. I drew the line when he wore them for a night mission; he objected and we got into a tussle about it.

Afterwards, I complained to Major Smith and when he called us together, the new medic said I just had an attitude because he was black. I said, "Fuck no, I just need

---

[4] Peter Dorland and James Nanney, Dustoff: Aeromedical Evacuation in Vietnam (Diane Pub Co; 1st Printing edition, April 1, 1982), p. 117, Center of Military History, United States Army, Washington, DC.

to know you're operating at peak performance, and when you inhibit your vision at night, purposefully, I can't trust you." Nothing was resolved. He went to Dau Tieng for a three-day stint and they ran into some heavy hot LZ pickups. When he returned, he asked for reassignment. I was glad to see him go. It wasn't his skin; it was his attitude.

We got a new pilot in once as a replacement for one who got combat wounded. This twenty-year-old new pilot was a hotdogger that the crew chiefs really fretted about, because they said he mistreated their choppers. I know of several times when he maxed out the torque indicator while recklessly taxiing down the runway. The chopper had to go immediately into the shop for repairs. Another time he took off from Lai Khe and hit the only tree left standing outside the perimeter after the Rome plows came. He said he'd wanted to "graze" the tree, but he hit it instead. Another time he did a low-level up Highway 13 from Saigon and pulled up too late and hit a US Army truck, smashing its windshield.

Eventually, the crew chiefs went to Maj. Smith and said they "quit" flying because of this new pilot. Smith said, "You can't quit, you're all volunteers." To which the crew chiefs said, "Okay, but we won't let him near our choppers, he's ruining them." The next week the pilot had orders to ship out.

When you're working with a team that's working in life-threatening situations, you need 100 percent complete trust. There can be no 99 percent; it has to be 100 percent. Our goal was to *complete* the mission, and anything that took away from that was unacceptable.

54 INCOMPLETE MISSIONS

I FLEW AS A DUSTOFF MEDIC FOR 15 months, mostly out of Lai Khe, Long Bien, Tan An, and Chu Lai. All decisions about where and when to land were worked out between the ground and our AC on the radio. The timing of the landing was usually decided by the people on the ground and revolved around whether they could spare the men to actually help load the patients or defend the LZ.

In hot LZs, sometime the ground radio people would ask us to hold off, but if there was a critically wounded GI who had to get to the hospital ASAP, we would override the ground decision to hold off, *but only* if they had personnel to help with the loading. We didn't like the ground making the decision about whether a pickup was "doable"—that was our decision. We knew what our chopper could and couldn't do. They could make a decision on assumptions only. The last thing the AC wanted was for his medic or crew chief to disconnect from the chopper intercom and go off on their own in a hot LZ. That could negatively affect our ability to perform future missions. In fact, the only reason I ever saw for an AC to postpone or decline a mission was if going in might prevent us from performing other missions in the next few hours. The logic being that getting shot down meant no more patients would get dusted off until a replacement Dustoff arrived (which could be many hours, depending on how many flyable choppers the Dustoff unit had and how far away they were.)

I recall a call we got once in Chu Lai during a typhoon. A patient had multiple gunshot wounds to the chest and legs and we had already received a "Notice" that choppers had been grounded. The winds and rain had arrived, but the eye of the storm was still some ways off, so the AC asked for volunteers to go for the pickup. I went and we did the mission. That was the only mission I remember where I had to slide the doors shut to keep out the weather. It was one hell of a ride.

Nui Ba Dinh, the Black Virgin Mountain near Tay Ninh

While I was at Lai Khe Dustoff there were four missions we could not complete and someone else had to be sent. The first was when we got lost in the fog and we had instrument failures up by the Cambodian border. The second and third happened when I was stationed at Dau Tieng. And the fourth occurred while stationed at Quan Loi, up near the Cambodian border.

We got a call for a pick up on Nui Ba Dinh, the Black Virgin Mountain, near Tay Ninh.

I had been reading Tolkien (author of *Lord of the Rings*) ravenously, so I came to call her The Lonely Mountain, since she was out in the plains all by herself. From Dau Tieng, we did have to fly over some razorback hills to get there, but they were nothing compared to this mountain. At the top the US had installed a bunch of communications equipment and established a permanent base. The supply road to the top was long and narrow in most places. In one place, there was a wide opening and a small field by the road halfway up. On this day, this location turned out to be the perfect spot for a VC booby trap.

We were on our way. There were two wounded, both shrapnel from a mine. A supply convoy was on its way to the top when the lead truck got hit by this mine. We came in and spotted the secure LZ, an open field right next to the blast. How convenient! We came in and were hovering at about 20 feet when there was an explosion. Later we learned it was an anti- helicopter IED, a jerry-rigged 105 round.

For me, two things happened. First, all sound ceased. Second, everything slowed down a lot. I checked the pilots, then the crew chief: *Good, everyone's ok*. I looked below and saw people laid out on the ground with lots of blood visible. Several warning indicator lights came on and the AC made a call to abort the pickup and get the chopper away from the people below.

Once we were away, he was looking for a place to set it down when I heard him say over the radio, "Aw, shit! Lai Khe Dustoff, this is Dustoff 48. We need a replacement Dustoff here at Black Virgin now. My chopper's blown and we may not make it back, over." He then asked the crew chief, "Whaddaya think?"

Tom replied, "I think we can make it, or at least try." So we flew the chopper back to Dau Tieng and landed on the airstrip. After shutdown, we looked over the chopper. Amazingly, every locked panel on the craft was blown open but the locks were still locked. After three hours Tom declared that the chopper was a "circle red x"—we could fly her back to Lai Khe for refit. When we got back to Lai Khe the AC told me to go get checked out at the hospital. So I went.

My ears were not working well; everything was faint. And there was this ringing. They checked me out and patched up my hand, which had gotten some shrapnel blown into it. The co-pilot, AC, and Tom were all okay.

The other mission we failed to complete was near Dau Tieng. I had forgotten about until the 2017 Vietnam Dustoff Association reunion in Dover, Delaware. My old crew chief, Tom Cash, was there and we started reminiscing. He asked me if I remembered a certain mission and I said, "No." He then went on and related his version. In his story he said, " . . . and I had to cut the cable" and all of a sudden, I remembered. I'll give you my version, then his to show how different perspectives can be, depending on which side of the helicopter you are on.

My recollection was we were coming in for a hoist mission and busy positioning the chopper. The ground had been bombed by B-52s and there wasn't a level place to set the chopper and load the patients who were on litters, so we hovered at about 40 feet and lowered our hoist.

There was a blast. I'm told it was an RPG that came in below us and exploded. The blast sucked our chopper down, then up and sideways. I heard Tom say, "I'm cutting the cable," and we flew away.

This is Tom's version: While we were hovering, the patient had been hooked up to the hoist cable and Tom was running the hoist to bring him up. There was a blast and the chopper went down then rose and went sideways. That motion started the hoist cable carrying the patient to swing and rotate, and in doing so the dangling patient swung around a dead tree. The patient got really hung up in the tree and after the GIs on the ground tried to free him, they waved us off. Then Tom said, "I'm cutting the cable," and then, "clear," and we took off—back first to Dau Tieng, then on to Lai Khe once a replacement chopper came in so we could replace the cut hoist cable.

The fact I never knew his side of the story was because we rarely, if ever, discussed missions once we got back, unless there was something to learn. I never asked why he cut the cable (I knew it had to be for a good reason and that was good enough for me), but it shows how two guys sitting in the back of a Dustoff each left that mission with different viewpoints that weren't cleared up for 48 years. Point of view matters.

Over the years, the hearing loss has definitely affected my life. I cannot hear high-pitched sounds, and when people speak, they use a lot of high-pitched sounds when using words that begin with p, c, f, j, k, q, s, t, and z. "Start" sounds like "heart," "bart," "cart," "mart," "dart," "fart" "part," or "tart," for example. It's even worse with any background noise, like in a restaurant with background music, or any noisy venue. Even a moderately-sized dinner party where more than one person is speaking at a time is too much for me. And speaking of music, I have come to realize that I don't like listening to music that has both instruments and singing.

Each interferes with the other. The exceptions are music I had heard before my hearing loss. Music afterwards can only be instrumentals or a cappella. When the two are combined, it's just noise to me.

My balance was also affected. After the war I went back to my old job as an ironworker and found quickly that I could not any longer walk steel during the erecting phase. I fell once from about ten feet and landed in a big pile of sand, luckily. My boss, Bill O'Brian, was very understanding and gave me a job running the "sit down drill." It was a three-feet high electric drill with a bicycle seat on top. I sat in the seat and used my weight to push big bolt holes through steel I-beams. It worked fine until I got through the steel and the drill just kept on going. My balance was such that I couldn't know when the drill slip from the bit going through the girder had begun. I had to quit my job.

I applied at the GM assembly plant and flunked their hearing test. No job. The same thing at the Chrysler plant. I ended up going to graduate school because the only thing I seemed able to do was work on the ground, like a desk job.

Then there is the ringing. After fifty years I have acclimated to it, except when the ringing changes pitch. It changes two or three times a year and I don't know why. That's a major reset and acclimation begins anew. It drives me nuts when I'm trying to go to sleep and have adopted a noisy fan that I use to create the white noise that can mask the ringing.

These are reminders, every day, of that event from so long ago. I was told later that the bomb was set to destroy the chopper. But the VC that set it off acted too soon because he was discovered. The blast ended up killing two soldiers on the ground and a lost leg for another. The patient whose pick up was delayed survived.

55 MOVING TO LONG BIEN

LAI KHE DUSTOFF WAS THE BEST YEAR OF my life. I was twenty-one years old. I had saved lives, I was a flight crewmember, and I'd become proud of myself. We were far from the Brass and inspections, and all the usual military *STRAC* stuff, like polished brass and boots, creased fatigues, and polished hooch floors. We were relaxed around our officers. Sure, we saluted and we maintained the chain of command, but we completed our missions without necessarily going by the book.

It was different when our unit was finally moved to Long Bien, near Saigon. At Lai Khe we mainly covered the 1st Infantry Division. (We also covered parts of the 25th Infantry, as well as parts of the 2nd Armored Division to our east near Di An). When the 1st Infantry Division moved out, the 1st Calvary Division moved in. The 1st Air Calvary had their own armed Medivacs and didn't need us. At Long Bien we would cover mostly the 9th Infantry Division and the Brown Water Navy. We were also right there next to Colonel Price, our company commander.

Colonels and Generals came and went every day. Our barracks were inspected, meaning we had to make our beds STRAC. Even when they weren't inspected, they were seen by general officers as they walked back and forth. We were no longer the kids who ran the block. You had to pay attention to what strange master sergeants said, who knew nothing about you, what you have been through and done, and they didn't even care. We were back in the regular Army now.

I was there for four months. I don't have many memories of the place, except small bits and pieces, like when we built our hooches and used *mahogany* threequarter plywood for the floors. Mahogany plywood? Really? The wood was beautiful, but once the floor was in place, we had to paint it gray! What a crime. We never painted our hooch floors in Lai Khe. I also recall something of a tiff about the new Nomex flight suits. These were fire-retardant clothing for the pilots, not the crews in the back. At one point, only the ACs could get them. The co-pilots didn't like that. Nobody asked us how we felt because it didn't matter; as long as we did what we were told. I also learned that it was Colonel Price who had turned down a Silver Star nomination for me, and his reasoning was: "because he was doing his job."

We covered mainly the southern areas into the Mekong Delta. Unlike where we had been stationed, where there were foothills, mountains, and rain forests. Now it was mostly rice paddies and tree-lined rivers. Our pilots had to invent new evasion f light maneuvers for avoiding ground fire. Up north we could use the trees to block the enemy's line of sight by staying at tree-top level, but not down in the Delta. The bottom line was, no matter the maneuver, you were more exposed to enemy rifle fire in the Delta. The best tactic was to gain altitude and get out of range at about 2,000 feet AGL (above ground level).

There was a lot more variety in the patients we picked up, too. Up north it was mainly Army and Special Forces units, with some LRRPs (Long Range Recon Patrols— who always seemed to wear the tiger-stripe camouflage fatigues), Montagnards, and Cambodian volunteers thrown in. I even picked up a Montagnard Princess once who was having difficulty in childbirth. When she was loaded, along with her husband, the future king of the tribe, he grabbed my arm as I reached for her and looked at me with a glare of "you better not."

Down south, there were more Australians, US Navy, Coast Guard, Korean, and ARVN troops, as well as the US Army soldiers. We even did pickups from Brown Water Navy boats (fast moving river patrol boats) and one Blue Water Navy destroyer.

The Delta was wet. All the time. You could tell when it was the "dry" season because the rivers were lower. Besides Dustoffs stationed at Long Bien, which was near Saigon, we also had a station down in the Delta. I cannot recall the name, but it may have been Tan An, which is half way to Can Tho where the 82 Dustoff Detachment was stationed. On a few occasions we and the 82nd worked the same battlefields at the same time. It was not a competition, although both units knew who the better unit was—we just didn't agree about that.

While stationed down there I had the occasion to witness the draining of a rice paddy. As the water receded, a group of Vietnamese youngsters walked into the paddy holding buckets and beating the water. When they got to my end they started reaching into the water and grasping fish barehanded and putting them in the bucket. I jumped up and started to help. I grabbed several fish, then reached down and grabbed another and OOW! My hand was pierced by a barb. They were small catfish. I pulled my hand out of the muddy water and pressed the wound to make it bleed. It hurt all the way to the bone in my hand. Damn. I stopped "fishing" and went and treated my wound. It never got infected and within a week it was like it never happened.

Next to that paddy was a small, dirt runway where we parked our chopper. One day, while waiting for a mission, we saw a small, funny-looking aircraft with really large wings circle the field. I figured the pilot needed to know what direction the wind was blowing so I went to our chopper and grabbed a smoke grenade. I popped it and let it roll away. As that happened the pilot was already on short approach to the runway at the other end and immediately gunned the engine and took off. He circled, we waved at him, and he came in and landed. He got out, walked over to us and demanded to know who threw that red smoke grenade! "I did," I said. He said, "You know RED means a hot LZ, right?" In all my experience we had landed lots of times at LZs, hot and cold, that used red smoke, as well as every other color. We never mentioned the color on the radio because the VC were listening and would pop the same color said on the airwaves. So we just told them to "pop smoke" and we'd tell them the color we saw. Sometimes it was red. So I told this civilian pilot I didn't know that. He was pissed. He was also not in any uniform, but he spoke like a colonel. He said he "ought to shoot" me but he "didn't have the time." He walked to the main base and a few hours later returned, got in the plane and took off.

The plane's side read, "Air America." We figured he was an ex-soldier now working for the CIA. The only time we saw those unique STOL planes (Short Take Off and Landing) was when we flew missions up near the Cambodian border. We saw them flying across the border all the time.

56 A FAKE SNAKE

THERE WAS ONE MISSION IN THE DELTA WORTH recalling. It was evening, near dusk, when we got a call for a snakebite. We went in, picked up the GI. He was on a litter. As we took off, I was, as usual, on alert for enemy fire. We started gaining altitude and I noticed a shed down on a paddy dike. It was dark against black as it was almost every night. Suddenly, I saw red dots forming at the shed. They didn't move. I was confused. First one, then another, then another.

Pretty soon there were seven or eight red dots just hanging there, glowing. I then realized they were tracers, and they were moving, straight for us! I yelled into my mic, "Dive and turn left— we're taking fire." As the co-pilot did so the helicopter thumped as some of the bullets hit us.

We got clear and I checked the patient. I couldn't find the bite mark. My Crew Chief, Richard Dean, was checking out our chopper, *Iron Butterfly II*. We knew we'd taken hits, just didn't know where. The AC kept an eye on the hydraulic pressures, while Dean and I checked out the back, including the patient. By this time the patient was really scared. He confessed to me that he faked the snakebite. It was his first night in the Delta and was scared. He didn't realize getting Dusted Off might be *more* dangerous.

I told the AC that the "patient" was a malingerer and that they ought to get the MPs to come pick him up, which they did. I also explained to him that by taking up our time we could not take any other missions that came in. And further, now that we had been shot up, the chopper would not be available for real patients tonight. We later discovered that none of the bullets that hit the chopper did any major damage and we stayed on station. One came up through the floor and took out part of the sole of Dean's left boot; another came up through the floor and passed through my Delaware Flag that I always carried with me and had been signed by everyone at Lai Khe Dustoff. The other three passed through without doing any damage.

We later did a calculation of how many shots were fired at us by counting the number of tracers I saw and multiplying by seven, since we believed that there were six regular bullets between each tracer. That adds up to fifty-six bullets coming at us, and only five hit us. We decided that whoever shot at us had a pretty good aim and could change clips pretty quickly.

And now for an unabashed advertisement. LTC. Steve Vermillion (Dustoff 48), one of our highly decorated ACs in the 4th Platoon, with whom I flew many times, wrote a book a while back. He asked me to edit it and it was a blast doing so. It's available online, just google the title and author. It's called *Dustoff*.

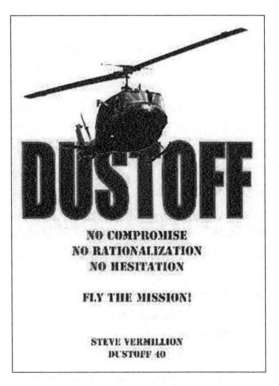

Steve is one of the ACs I flew with, both at Lai Khe and in Long Bien. He wrote this book. Pretty cool.

57 THE WORST OF THE WAR PORN

I FLEW A LOT OF MISSIONS FOR THE 4th Platoon and I have refrained from writing about every single one that impacted me one way or another. I call it "war porn" if I get into describing in too much detail some of the shit I've seen, treated, and dealt with while having a job of trying to keep people from dying. But I do want to write a few sentences about several pickups to just give some suggestion.

We went just south of Lai Khe to an area known as Ben Cat on a night mission to pick up a wounded Special Forces soldier in September 1968. Locating hot LZs at night is a bit difficult. You know Charlie (VC) is listening to your communications, so a lot is left unsaid, such as the kind of light or strobe being used at night. You let them turn it on, then you tell them what you see. This night we didn't see a light, they didn't have one, so they directed us in by the sound of our chopper in a game of "warm-cold."

Then we were told we were right over them, so we circled around and came down. We were at a hover at a clearing in the woods, maybe 30 feet off the ground. We had visual contact and began to land. As I was looking outside to help with the landing, I saw white flashes and tracers coming at us from right next to the troops we were trying to approach, maybe twenty feet away. We took hits and everybody on the ground scrambled and told us to scram. We did, but the chopper was sluggish, and we called Lai Khe Dustoff and said we may be going down. Our AC really nursed that machine, and in a few minutes we made it back to our LZ in the base.

Right next to us was Fourth Up cranking their Dustoff to come get us. Technically there is no Fourth Up—these guys had had the night off and had been drinking some, or more. But they came anyway. Ya gotta love them for that.

We found out there were "spider holes" at the LZ. Once the US forces had cleared them out, First Up went and did the pickup.

I remember one night at Lai Khe I was on my cot reading. Then I heard a whistling sound overhead. A while later I heard a faint *Boom, Boom, Boom* to the east and shortly thereafter I heard a louder and closer *Blam, Blam, Blam* to the west. I knew the battleship *USS New Jersey* was on station off the coast, and I have assumed all this time I was hearing her fire at some enemy. But in researching this note, I have discovered that while the . was off the coast of Phan Thiet, almost due east of us at that time, her 16-inch gun range fell far short of where we were. We were about 100 miles west of the *New Jersey*, and her gun range was about 22 to 25 miles. So all these years I had thought I had heard the *New Jersey* firing and now I have to report that it was some other artillery firing.

What I was most curious about it at the time was the fact that I heard the shells passing overhead before any reports of their being fired. This told me a couple of things: first the rounds being fired are supersonic, and second, the rounds were not that far overhead when they passed. The third thing I just realized is that the target was actually pretty close to Lai Khe. Just sayin'.

I have only heard one B52 raid, even though there were hundreds of raids by these bombers, and I have viewed them in the air from tens of miles away. They are a fearsome display of power. I was again in my cot at Lai Khe, fast asleep. Now back then, I was a deep sleeper. If I was woken up abruptly, it took me a while to get my bearings. This night I was fast asleep, then suddenly found myself on the floor and hearing a tremendous barrage of bombs fall. Our canvas tent was flapping in every direction as the rapid changes in air pressure pushed the fabric around. Then it stopped.

By then I was fully awake and wondering what the hell just happened. All of us were wondering this. One of the officers came in smiling and asked us if we liked that. Then he told us it scared the bejeezes out of everyone in the RTO, and 1st Division HQ called us to tell us it was a B52 raid "not far off." The only way I can imagine I ended up on the floor was that I was bounced out of my cot by the first blasts. I weighed 200 pounds at the time, so that was no small feat.

Another time down at Long Bien we heard on the radio that a helicopter had just crashed out on the perimeter of the base. We went to see if we could help and when we arrived the chopper was in flames. I saw two people crawl out of the flames. They were both on fire. One collapsed but the other kept crawling, ever slower, then stopped and collapsed. It was absolutely awful—an image that hasn't diminished over 50 years. At the time I was told that our choppers, the UH-1H, were made of magnesium and they burned really easily. Later I discovered that the UH-1B models did have *some* magnesium components, but our newer "H" models had none; they were all aluminum.

There was another time down in the Mekong Delta we were flying back from the hospital after a mission when we received a call about a plane going down nearby. We got the coordinates and plotted a path there. It was a big open swamp. We circled around for a while, and another aircraft arrived too. We chatted for a while and decided that the swamp had sucked them up and there were no survivors. There was not even a visible impact area. I had a hard time believing a plane could disappear like that until that Valuejet crashed in the Everglades in 1996. Then I became a believer. But for family survivors of the Mekong crash, it must have been hard: no body, no plane, nothing, just gone.

We also did a hoist pick up off of a US Navy vessel once. The ship had a lot of antennas and there was no way we could land. So we hoisted the patient aboard. That's pretty tricky flying. The ship is moving and the chopper is tracking it. But the ship is also going up and down due to wave action. Catching the hoist after it was lowered required more slack than usual because of this wave action. They attached the Stokes Litter (a metal litter) to our cable and we hauled him up. Those antennae were a worry the whole time.

There was another hoist we did in a hot LZ up near Quan Loi. It was another Stokes Litter lift, but our hoist motor stopped with the patient halfway up to us. We started taking fire and I could see where the shots came from. I grabbed my Car-15 and, after the patient swung out of the way, I opened fire. The AC gained altitude, but this made the litter continue to swing.

Every time he swung out of the way I opened up. From the patient's viewpoint it must have looked like I was shooting at him. Neither he nor we took hits. We flew all the way back to Quan Loi with him dangling about 35 feet below us. The hoist was on the crew chief's side, so he controlled the cable as much as possible. The landing was delicate as we had to gently land the litter first. That was done by us in the back giving the AC second-by-second instructions until he was down. Once out of the way, we came in and landed gently to ensure that loose cable didn't go somewhere we didn't want it to go.

As we exited the chopper, an ABC news film team came up to us and wanted an interview. When they came to me, I put my hands up and said, "No can do. My Mom doesn't even know I am flying." When I got home the next year, Mom said she saw me, and that she first recognized me by my walk. She was watching the news one night and she yelled at Dad, "That's Larry's walk!" They paid attention and they saw me in the background while someone else was interviewed.

It never does any good to lie to your Mom; she's gonna find out anyway. And I never knew I had "a walk."

58 BIG DECISIONS IN SPRING OF '69

IT WAS SPRING 1969. I'D BEEN THERE ABOUT 18 months and I had some decisions to make. My extended tour in Vietnam was winding down. If I went back to the States, I would have to spend a full year at some Army base where everyone worried about how shiny their boots were and whether their bed was *STRAC*. I did not want to spend a year worrying if my socks were folded correctly or placed in the correct order in the top shelf of my footlocker. I liked the relative freedom of working "In Country" and I longed for the relaxed atmosphere of a more forward unit, far away from the Generals and the garritroopers (those not quite at the front or the rear, in terms of command).

So, I extended my tour again by another six months. Of course, there were a few carrots in the deal for me. First, I would get another free 30-day leave, all travel expenses paid; and second, I would get another 7-day R&R. Plus, since my return date to the States was now in January 1970, and my DEROS date (Date Eligible to Return from Over Seas) was May 4, 1970, the four months I would be back in the States would be forgiven, and I would get an "early out" in January.

At the same time I was negotiating this, I was also approached by an officer from the 44th Medical Brigade HQ who asked if I would consider re-upping for another three years in the Army. If I did, he said, they would give me a $10,000 bonus and make me a 1st Lieutenant. I had just made Sp5 two months earlier, and here they were talking about moving me up from the pay grade of E-5 to O-2—a jump of six paygrades. I thought about it for about 30 seconds, then said "No." I did not want to become a "lifer," a 20-year man who retires at age 40 and moves to Arizona. So, I signed the six-month extension for In Country, on the stipulation that I would be sent to a more forward Dustoff unit. (Little did I know that the unit I was sent to had been wiped out twice over the past eighteen months and spent nine months with just three functioning choppers instead of the usual six.) But first, I had my 30-day leave coming up.

I then devised a 30-day leave that started in Borneo and ended up in Bangkok. My brother, Leslie Kipp, was in the Peace Corps in Sarawak, Borneo, only 500 miles from where I was in 'Nam. I got tickets organized and flew from Saigon to Bangkok, then to Singapore, then to Brunei. Les met me at Brunei and he took me to his place nearby in Limbang, Sarawak. I had brought two cans of Hamms Beer from the Saigon Px with me. We got to his place and put them in his kerosene refrigerator, which I had never heard of and thought was cool, then we left and went out and checked out the town and some of his local friends. When we got back the beer was cool and we opened, toasted and drank. Ewwww. It was 3.2 beer, kinda flat and pretty tasteless. Les then went and opened the only beer available in Sarawak: Guinness Stout, warm. For me, it was wicked, but it was all we had, so I drank it.

The next day Les told me to "wait by that tree" and when he came back, we were going up river for an overnight. I waited. And waited. I placed my hand on the tree trunk and leaned against it, still waiting. Instead of botanizing, I was just observing... everything. I wanted to take it all in. Borneo! It was on my Bucket List. Suddenly I felt a stinging on the hand I was using to lean against the tree. I looked and it was covered in ants; biting ants. I then realized they were also on my arm, and then my neck, and my chest, and back. I flung off my shirt and began brushing off the biting ants. There were hundreds of them. About then my brother shows up and wonders what I'm doing. When told he laughed, and said, "You shoulda asked me." Sure.

We each had our packs, and we went over to the river, which had a steep embankment going to a very small "dock." The steps down to the dock were cut into a log. My feet are size 13, so I had to be careful that I actually placed each foot on each step. By the time I got to the bottom, another longboat (a dugout canoe that's pretty long) pulled up with several 60-pound bags of rice. I watched as locals rushed down the steps, loaded a bag on their back and nearly ran up the steps with it. I was impressed with their strength, dexterity, and ease of movement. It was like poetry in motion. Each body movement had a purpose; there were no useless movements.

Then it was our turn to get in that same boat. It was made of a single log. The inside was about fourteen inches wide with slats placed for seats. You always had to have your balance, no exceptions. We got in, loaded the supplies Les needed for the project he was working on upstream, and took off. I was in front and my brother handed me an eight-foot pole. "What's that for?" I asked. "To beat off the crocodiles we might otherwise run over," he said. "If you see one, just poke it." Borneo crocs I learned later were legend—extremely big and aggressive.

We took off up the Limbang River. I noticed an 80 hp. outboard mounted on the back with a five-foot long prop shaft. Interesting, just like the ones I saw in Thailand. We motored up the river for an hour, then Les told me to notice a particular tree. "Okay," I said, and on we went. The river was very curvy. An hour later Les tapped me on the shoulder and pointed to a tree. It was the same tree, only this time we were fifty yards on the other side of it. That's how meandering the river was. As we went up river at about 10 mph, I was botanizing all the way, checking out the nifty butterflies, birds, and land mammals, all the while looking for crocs. For all I know, we may have nearly run over some that I missed, these other views were so enticing.

Gradually the bank sides began to grow. By the time we reached our destination, the last human village on that river, the banks were twenty-five feet above us, and the trees another 200 to 300 feet higher. The dock, which did not stick out very far, was just as tall. When we landed, we had to climb a ladder up to the dock. I asked Les why the dock was so high, and he said, "It's low water. If it rains here or up river, the river will rise all the way up, even with the dock, in a matter of two hours." Dang.

We had arrived at an Eban tribal village. The longhouse was built on stilts with the f loors about five feet above ground level. There was another log staircase leading up to the longhouse where everybody lived. We entered and there was the Chief. Les introduced me. The Chief said something to Les, and Les said, "They want to know why you didn't bring your helicopter with you." I said, "Tell him I cannot fly it over water." He did, and that was a satisfactory answer.

I discovered the longhouse was one big apartment. The ceiling was probably ten feet above the floor and shingled in thatch. The longhouse was probably 25 feet wide and maybe 100 feet long. Interior thatch walls marked off each family's living space with a five-foot wide walkway down the middle. The entry area, on both sides, belonged to the Chief and his extended family—about 20 extended families lived in it. The first thing I noticed was a poster of JFK on the wall. We settled in the Chief's area for the night.

The next morning Les told me that I cannot help with the well digging project he was helping the Eban with. "They need to learn all the tasks; if you help, they won't learn that." So, I made myself a peanut butter sandwich for lunch and decided to go out botanizing. It was a great place to do that. The trees! They looked to be 200 feet high, if not higher. I had never seen trees so high, at least from the ground. I thought about some of our hoist missions in Vietnam and tried to make a comparison, but I couldn't.

We were on one side of the river, so I had a choice of about 180 degrees as to where I wanted to start. I decided to go up along the river, then circle back around and come in from the downstream end. I took off, just gazing, stopping to investigate something up close, then moved on to the next amazing thing. I was surprised at just how bare the bottom of this huge forest was. Most of the interesting things were up in the trees. Including the sounds. I assumed some of the sounds I heard were from insects, some from birds, some from frogs, and some, perhaps, from arboreal primates. I wandered all morning, just following my nose.

Eventually the ground began to get soggy, and trees began to get shorter. Then I came upon a soggy, almost swampy area with the trees sparse and very short, maybe only 30 feet high. I saw one that looked like a good climbing tree where I could sit down and eat my lunch. I made my way up it, after checking for ants, and found a nice large limb on which to spread out my lunch and lean back against the trunk. Ants don't like swampy areas much. It was awesome. The sun was overhead now, so I knew it was around noon, even though I didn't have a watch.

I decided I should begin making my way back when I realized that I didn't know from which way I had arrived! I stopped, lit a cigarette, and thought about this for a moment. *Okay, don't panic,* I thought. I had no clue how I arrived at that tree. *No clue.* I waited for something to come to me. In the process, I smoked about five cigarettes. Over an hour passed as I waited for an idea. I was now worried. I hadn't noted the direction of the sun when I began my trip, so I couldn't use the sun's position as a guide. Damn! I also remember Les telling me that this was the last village on the river. We would have to go 500 miles further to run into any other towns or villages if we kept heading in the upstream direction. I couldn't just pick any direction and start going; to do so would probably get me lost, permanently. So, what did I know? I knew we had headed upstream, so downstream would be the way to go, kinda. I knew that the Limbang River was nearby, so if I walked North (downstream) and found a stream, then followed it downstream to the Limbang, then walked up the Limbang to the village . . . no, that was too complicated. Damn!

I was finishing another cigarette when all of a sudden, I heard a new sound in the forest.

My ears perked up, I turned toward it, and then, *there!* I saw it. It was a chicken scratching around the forest floor. I knew all chickens were domesticated, so *that* chicken belonged to someone. All I had to do was follow that chicken and it would lead me to people. At last, a plan.

As I climbed down the tree, I noticed the chicken tended to move away from me and get lost in the foliage and brush. I then realized that I had two tasks to do: 1) Follow that chicken, and 2) Don't get so close that I interfere with its normal movements. That's what I did all afternoon: smoked cigarettes and followed that chicken. I did not botanize.

Eventually the light began to fade a bit. Then I heard someone chopping wood. People! Great, I walked toward the chopping sound and found myself in an area where the big trees had been cut (by the Eban I learned later) and young saplings were now growing. There was a woman chopping a sapling to become firewood after drying. She looked up and saw me and she turned white. The chicken ran off between her and me and I just raised my hand, smiled, and waved and kept going toward the clearing I saw up ahead. I later learned that I had scared the bejeezes out of the woman, who thought I was a ghost, which they naturally believe in.

As I approached the longhouse, Les came running. He said, "Where the hell have you been?!" I told him I went out for a walk since there was nothing for me to do in the village. He was beside himself. He thought I was lost and was preparing to organize a search party. I said I was lost but that chicken over there, and I pointed at it, showed me the way back. Les explained that to the tribesmen who were gathered, and in their language too! They all laughed and welcomed me back. Since then, the term "bird brain" doesn't mean the same thing as it used to.

59 PARTY WITH THE NATIVES

THAT NIGHT THE EBANS HELD A PARTY IN our honor. I never got a count of how many people lived there but it seemed to me it was about 15-20 extended families. I recall seeing a large radio in the Chief's area, and Les told me that these people knew Kennedy had been assassinated about two hours after it happened. We both wondered at the way technology was making the world smaller. And as I said, right there on the wall was a poster of JFK. I got the impression these people liked Kennedy, and they certainly liked Les, who spoke their language and was teaching them how to build a well so they had clean drinking water close by.

The river water was close, but it was also variable in its clarity and availability. If the water was low, you had to go down and risk the crocodiles, then carry the small amount of water back up that steep incline. If the water was high, it was often tea colored or muddy and probably not potable. So the well seemed to be a good solution. But it was important they learned how to build the well themselves, so that when they moved (because they were hunter-gatherer type people, kinda), they could take that knowledge with them.

It was likely that they'd move at some point. They did slash and burn agriculture. They would cut some trees and create an open area, then grow upland, or dryland rice. The forest would quickly regrow and I guess it was easier to fell a few large trees (these were upwards of 200 feet tall) than to clear the regrowth. Besides, the logs from the trees made great dugout canoes, another resource.

I mentioned crocodiles. There are two kinds in Borneo: the smaller, freshwater Siamese crocodile, and the larger saltwater crocodile. I am referring to the larger ones. Males can get up to 17 feet long and weight up to 2,200 lbs. They move fast—up to 17 mph in the water.

They are formidable. In Borneo, attacks by these scary things are common. Les told me that the members of this village had made "peace" with the crocs a while back after an interesting thing happened. Apparently, the village had captured and killed a crocodile. A while later the small daughter of the Chief went missing. A few days later she was found alive, and she said she had been captured by the king of the crocodiles and he was going to kill her because the village had killed his daughter. The girl said that if he let her go, she would go back to the village and tell them he had let her go on the condition that there would be no more killing on either side. The village discussed this story and they decided not to hunt the crocodiles any more. And since that time, there have been no more incidents with the crocodiles. Les said that the little girl's story was completely believable based on their belief system of ghosts and spirits. I believe they are some sort of animists and accept that every living thing has a spirit.

Which gets me to headhunting. A while back, James Brooke, the first "White Rajah," had come to Sarawak, Borneo, looking for adventure. When he deposed the local pirates with his yacht's 2-pound cannon on its bow, the local Sultan of Brunei declared him Monarch of Sarawak in 1841. Brooke's family ruled Sarawak until they ceded it to England in 1946. So they ruled Sarawak for 105 years!

Somewhere along the line, one of the White Rajahs forbade any more headhunting by the local population. It was explained to me that headhunting was kind of like getting a high school or college letter. If you owned someone's head, you owned their soul, and that meant more power and prestige for you. Anyway, the headhunting stopped, until World War II when the Japanese invaded Borneo. It turned out that Brunei, a very small Sultanate, seems to have all the oil of the big island of Borneo, and the oil in Brunei is very clean. So clean that it can be burned in ship boilers without going to a refinery. Japan's Imperial Navy wanted this oil, and all the other oil in the region to wage their wars after the US cut off their oil supplies. So, after they invaded the Philippines they went on south and took over all the oil fields of the Dutch Indies and Brunei.

With the arrival of the Japanese, the locals felt that it was a good time to bring back headhunting, which they did. A lot of Japanese soldiers and sailors lost their heads there.

So anyway, the Eban were going to have a party for us. Now everybody in the world has an alcoholic beverage. I just didn't know that what they offered me was alcoholic, it didn't smell that way. I don't even know what it was, but I think it was some sort of mild hallucinogenic substance that was chewed so the saliva could break it down chemically, then spit back out and allowed to ferment for a while. Making this stuff was apparently a social thing. Well, it got me. That's why I can't tell you too much about the party. I did not notice any taste of alcohol.

Having nearly killed myself eight months before by getting blind drunk, I was repulsed by the odor of alcoholic drinks. This beverage had no such odor. I remember laughing and talking; of course Les had to translate everything I said for them, and vice versa, so things took a little longer. But I do remember that we all wanted to have a good time. I certainly did.

At some point my mind got fuzzy and I laid back on what I thought were some fishing nets. As everyone else was talking and laughing, I was trying to take stock of my brain. I was laid back looking up. Then I noticed these Japanese glass fishing f loats hanging in a net from the ceiling. I remembered seeing these as a kid at and near Fenwick Island in Delaware back in the 1950s. I was told they were floats used by the Japanese to keep their nets in order while fishing, and every once in a while one would get loose and wander up on our shoreline here on the East Coast. They were greenish or bluish colored transparent globes of very thick glass that would on occasion wash up on the shore. This is what was going through my mind while I examined these globes. Then I realized they were skulls!

Oh my god! Here I am drunk and I'm gonna be up there next! "Les!" I called for help. Then I passed out and didn't wake up till the next morning. The next morning everyone was smiling and laughing, I thought at me, but my head was clear. No hangover. The day was bright and suddenly everything was cool.

60 BARKING LIZARDS

WE SPENT A FEW MORE DAYS THERE WITH Les working on the well, and me off by myself since my "help" was not going to be needed. I was more careful in my walks and I did a lot of botanizing. What was really great was that there were no VC in the vicinity, though my guard never went completely away.

Finally, it was time for us to head back down river. The plan was to go past the next village downstream, where I had seen a log half-chopped and shaped into a dugout still up on two short logs, and get to the government bungalow where we were to meet a Malaysian Park Ranger for some reason. We got in our dugout and off we went, Les in the back running the outboard and me in front with my pole. A while after we took off it started to rain. It really rained. I had to bail out the dugout, which turned out to be a good thing because the rain got really cold. I was surprised at how cold it was.

We came upon the village with the half-completed dugout and Les pulled in. We lashed up our narrow dugout next to the half-completed one. It was bigger—a good 40 inches wide and 30 feet long. We hid under it for shelter from the rain. We were soaked, and I was cold. I'm used to thunderstorms, where the storm rolls in, it rains and thunders for a while, then moves on.

Not this one. It was completely clouded over and the rain just poured down. Then it started to rain harder. But in another hour it petered out and we got back in our boat and headed downstream.

We pulled up to this dock, lashed the dugout, unloaded our stuff, and trudged into this nice cabin. It was a newer, government-built cabin with a magnificent front porch, and inside the hall was at least 15 feet wide with two bedrooms on each side of the hall. In the back was the kitchen and another porch. No running water, just a hand pump.

The Ranger shows up and he and Les have a happy reunion. Soon, we were warm again and some food was set out on the table in the dining area of the kitchen. No windows, just screens. In the back the area was cleared for maybe fifty yards, and on either side and in the far back the trees went up 200 feet at least. While the Ranger (sorry, I cannot recall his name) and Les were talking about local stuff in Malay, I guess, I was just checking this guy out and eating my dinner. He seemed trustworthy.

I heard a dog barking out back. I interrupted their conversation to say that I didn't recall seeing a dog when we arrived. "That's not a dog," the Ranger said in perfect British-accented, English.

"What is it?" I asked.

"It's a lizard," he said. Now this bark was not a squeak. It was the bark of a big dog, like maybe a Saint Bernard. Well, I learned that lizards get pretty big in Sarawak. These were water monitor lizards and can get up to nine feet long. *And they bark.* The Ranger told me they are quite fast. He said once they get going they rise up on their hind legs and run on just the back legs. I learned earlier with the Portuguese Man of War not to make assumptions about wildlife. I imagined a situation where I saw one of these dragons running at me full tilt and got a shudder down my spine.

We weren't far from the equator, and that meant 12-hour days. It started getting dark and by the time we finished with the dishes, it was night. The jungle around us changed. It got louder. A gazillion different kinds of crickets, frogs, and other peepers, chirpers, and buzzers filled the night air with their song. It was a lot like Lai Khe at night, only louder.

We moved to the front porch and the conversation turned to ghosts. Everybody in Borneo believes in ghosts in one form or another. In fact, there are areas of Borneo that remained uninhabited because everybody agreed that land belonged to the ghosts. I'm sure the timber companies have put that belief to good use over the past fifty years (sigh).

Then they told me a ghost story. The Ranger and Les had been at this cabin about four months earlier. It was just the two of them and eventually they each went to their bedrooms and called it a night. Les said that later he heard someone walk up the steps, walk across the porch, and open the door. Les got out of bed and walked to his door and opened it just after this visitor had opened the front screen door. As Les came out of his bedroom, the Ranger came out of his bedroom, on the opposite side of the hall. They were startled and confused, looking for the visitor. All they found was each other.

We made it down to Limbang the next day and the day after that we flew to Kuching, a "major" town on the way to Singapore. Les had some Peace Corps business to do, but it all got delayed because Les got ill. He had a moderate fever and no desire to do anything.

He rebuffed my offers of help and said he would work through it. "Go out and enjoy the town," he said. Convinced he wasn't going to die, I did what he asked and I botanized the entire walkable area, ran into a black pepper farm, and learned that "tea" is pronounced "tey" and that "tea with sugar" is pronounced "tey-o." No coffee, but I still had my caffeine fix.

After three days Les got better and we moved on to Singapore. We entered this hotel and the young lady taking the registration information spoke perfect British English. No accent. I had to give them my home address for some reason and as soon as I said "Delaware" she blurted out, "Delaware! You have three counties, New Castle, Kent, and Sussex, your capital is Dover, your largest city is Wilmington, and I bet your father works for the Dupont company." She had the most gracious smile. Then I got a hold of myself and admitted to her that yes, my Dad was a chemist for the Dupont company. She was tickled pink.

Les and I toured Singapore, him giving me history lessons with every turn of a corner. He knew a lot about World War II and what happened here in Singapore during that time.

The next day we took a train from Singapore to Bangkok. Les is also a train expert, especially, then, about steam engines. Our train was pulled by a 2-6-2! I learned that meant two guide wheels in the front (one on each side), six power wheels in the middle, and two guide wheels under the cab. When we arrived, they were loading the tender car (that carries the fuel) with logs. It was a wood-burning steam locomotive. I had only seen coal and oil burners, never a wood burner. Cool. The train took off and I ended up spending the whole day leaning out the window botanizing as much as I could.

The next morning we arrived in Hat Yai, Thailand, where we got off and spent a few days. We stayed at the train station hotel, which I discovered had been set up by the British, so they served continental breakfasts of toast, tea, and marmalade. I hate marmalade, but that was all they had. It was in this town I learned about tropical fruits and nuts. It was the cashew harvest season, and everyone had fivepound bags of fresh or roasted cashews for sale for about 35¢. I ate several bags in the three days I was there. They also had this thing called rambutan. Later I found out here it's called "hairy fruit." It's a ping-pong-ball sized red fruit with green, thick "hairs" coming out of it. You pull open the skin and inside is a delicious grapelike fruit, only drier. I also discovered the Frankenstein of all fruits, the durian. This is a 9-pin ball sized fruit that looks like the mace weapon. You can smell it a block away and it smells like it should be burned. Les says it fills the place of cheese for Asian diets, since most Asians don't like, or eat milk products, except ice cream.

We got back on the train and headed for Bangkok. Les met up with some Peace Corp friends he'd trained with and I went back to visit the Teacher.

When it was time to head back to 'Nam, Les gave me two weapons he had obtained in Borneo: a 150-pound pull crossbow and an 8-foot-long poison dart blowgun. When I got back to Long Bien, I wanted to try out the crossbow. The string was set by holding the string with both hands and using your feet to push the bow away from you. It was hard. I took one of the arrows and some friends got a piece of the three-quarter-inch mahogany plywood still lying around and I aimed and fired it. The bamboo arrow went through the plywood! I imagined this cross bow was similar to the ones the VC had used back in 1965 and 66 when Dustoffs would return with arrows stuck in them. I fired the blowgun too. I had to be careful, because the accompanying bamboo quiver was filled with lethal, poisoned arrows. It was used to shoot monkeys in the jungle.

61   HEAD IN THE CLOUDS

I HAD JUST A COUPLE OF WEEKS LEFT before I was to go up north to my new unit. There were missions to fly and we took them as they came. By now I thought of myself as an "old hand" at this job, yet we were still young. You do have to remember that the AC was probably 20 or 21, the co-pilot was 19, and the crew in the back was 18 to 20, and here we were in a 4.7-million- dollar aircraft with no one looking over our shoulders. We had a lot of fun flying in them when there wasn't a mission to do, like empty return flights. Low levels were the most common, and just thrilling.

Once we were on our way back from dropping off a patient at a surgical hospital in the Delta. We were headed north to Long Bien when the AC said matter-of-factly, "See that cloud?" as he pointed to a small cumulus cloud in front of us. You could see that it had started to rise. "I wonder how high we'll have to get in order to fly over it," he quipped. The co-pilot said, "Let's find out," and we were off. We climbed. I watched the ground below become less defined, roads turned into lines, rivers into brown ribbons. And we climbed more. I looked over the AC's shoulder out the front windshield and the cloud top was still far away, and higher than it had been. Soon, the sound of the rotorblades began to thin out. I was looking out my side smoking my cigarette. I took a drag and no smoke. I relit my cigarette and took a puff. When I puffed again, no smoke. My cigarette was out. I asked the AC what our elevation was, and he said 17,000 feet. We were still below that cloud's top. We continued to climb. Then, Paddy Control, the Air Control station for our area, got on the horn and said, "Unidentified aircraft at 20,000 ASL near xRay Sierra 750300, please identify."

The co-pilot looked at the map and said to the AC, "That's us." The AC replied, "Paddy Control, this is Dustoff 49, over."

There was a pause. Then "Uhh, Dustoff 49 are you a fixed wing? Over." The AC replied, "Paddy Control, that's a negative, over."

Paddy replied "Uh, Dustoff 49, you're not rated at over 10,000, and you're twice that. Be advised, we have a flight of B52s coming through your area in five—that's five minutes—over. Recommend you descend. Over."

Our AC said, "Roger Paddy Control, Dustoff 49 signing off, over." Then we started going down. We looked at the cloud and it had begun to anvil out. We concluded that it was at about 35,000 to 40,000 feet elevation. Dang, didn't make it. We also had to f ly around this "cell" due to the rain coming down. I have talked with people later and related this story and some have remarked that it's amazing we were not all blacked out due to lack of oxygen. The dead cigarette was the clue. I would still like to fly over a cloud like that in a helicopter.

62 THE 54TH

ON JUNE 13, 1969, I ARRIVED IN CHU Lai almost two years into my tour.

The 54th Medical Detachment was different. Normally Army units are organized as Squad, Platoon, Company, Brigade, Regiment, Division, Corps. Detachments are formed when there's a need to create a unit out of existing units and "detach" them from the normal chain of command to do a specific job. I had never been in a Detachment unit before, so I had to become familiar with the similarities and differences from my experience in the 4th Platoon of the 45th Medical Company. The first thing I was told was that the unit had been wiped out two times over the past 18 months.

In my research for this section I found the following worth presenting here:[5]

From Senate Bill 2268 presented in the 144th Congress (never passed).

(13) the 54th Medical Detachment typified the constant heroism displayed by Dust Off crews in Vietnam, over the span of a 10-month tour, with only 3 flyable helicopters and 40 soldiers in the unit, evacuating 21,435 patients in 8,644 missions while being airborne for 4,832 hours;

(14) collectively, the members of the 54th Medical Detachment earned 78 awards for valor, including 1 Medal of Honor, 1 Distinguished Service Cross, 14 Silver Star Medals, 26 Distinguished Flying Crosses, 2 Bronze Star Medals for valor, 4 Air Medals for valor, 4 Soldier's Medals, and 26 Purple Heart Medals;

(1) the 54th Medical Detachment displayed heroism on a daily basis and set the standard for all Dust Off crews in Vietnam;

---

[5] Congressional Bills 114th Congress, From the U.S. Government Publishing Office, S. 2268 Introduced in Senate (IS), https://www.govinfo.gov/content/pkg/BILLS-114s2268is/html/BILLS-114s2268is.htm

54th Medical Detachment (Helicopter Ambulance) patch

During my flying with the unit, I did not get the feeling that many of the pilots had been there very long. I also learned that the I Corps had units I had never worked with, like the US Marines.

When I first arrived, I was struck by our compound. At camp there was a rather ornate duck pond with a bridge over it made of concrete and wood. I was told that it was added-to every time someone got an Article 15. In addition to a few ducks, the unit had a pig they bought as a youngster. As time passed, it never grew up. We learned it was a Vietnamese pot-bellied pig, which don't get large. One day several of the guys took the pig to a farmer to have it bred. They came back red-faced but laughing. When I asked what happened, they told me about the pidgin English conversation they had and tried to explain to the farmer that they wanted our pig bred with a boar of a larger size. The farmer, once he realized what we wanted, started to laugh. They finally learned that our pig was a "boy-san," a male pig.

Chu Lai was different. We were right on the coast. Our location was almost next to a cliff that had a walkway that went down to the beach. I made use of it several times. Besides the beach, there was a small barrier-like coral reef filled with nifty looking fish, urchins, and starfish. The beach was long and almost flat, backstopped by the cliffs. At low tide I would walk out to where the water would just cover my ears but not my nose when I lay down. I soaked up the warm sun and the cool waters and often fell asleep. I'd wake up later when the tide had risen up to my nose. The beach was curious in one respect. Some of the rounded stones in the sand, when wet, looked like the Cats Eyes I had seen in Bangkok. I regret I never collected any of them, though I did give them a good look. The walk down was always nice too. The weeds there were a tropical butterfly weed and always seemed in bloom. The area was sort of arid, so the plants were not robust, but they did bloom, and I always stopped to look at them on the way down and back up.

One day, one of the ACs said he was going to fly out "to this island off the coast" and check it out. "Anybody want to come along?" he asked. Several of us jumped at the chance. It was, maybe a twenty-minute flight to the island. The island was volcanic and called Cu Lao Re. We landed on a beach that stretched a long ways to the sea and was backstopped by a volcanic cliff. For some reason the silhouette of the island as we approached has stuck in my mind. It had a cone shape in the middle. This memory came in handy in 2016, when I revisited the island, but that's another story.

When we got out of the chopper I looked up and the cliff actually curved overhead. Technically, we were under the top of the cliff. Cool. We all went our different ways. I was interested in checking out the beach and the coral barrier reef beyond it. It was amazing.

Everything caught my eye. I went into botanizing mode and stayed in it for hours. There was an inner and an outer reef that the waves crashed upon. In between was a canyon of seawater filled with every imaginable tropical fish there could be. I said to myself, "This is straight out of National Geographic!" There were big fish, small fish, and tiny fish, all made of these wondrous colors! I saw starfish like none I had seen before. I wanted to swim in the canyon, but the wave action was pretty active; besides I have a fear of sharks. Being in, or near, their environment was not to my liking. So I looked from above down into the water.

The tide was out so some of the inner coral barrier became walkable. I looked at everything, a small pool with a shrimp-like creature in it, a lobster walking in the canyon, sea urchins of unique design and color left high and dry, starfish huddling in a small pool, then...there it was! A giant clam imbedded in the coral. This critter was three feet from stem to stern. There was a blue felt-like ribbon along the entire length of each half of each half-shell. I learned later these were eyes, or more specifically, photoreceptors. The clam was open about an inch and I presumed it was feeding by sucking the water and filtering it. It was stunning.

I came to the end of the coral reef and walked back to the beach, which was now covered by the water a little more. I was near the cliff still, but about a mile, I guess, down from where we landed. It was rockier here and I had to watch my step some. Then, I saw what looked like an opening into the cliff. I picked up speed and came to an overhang that went into the cliff. Cool, a cave! I walked in, slowly, cautiously, wondering if there were any critters in there I should worry about. Then I saw light. It was a burning candle, then two, then more.

I realized this was human occupied. As I turned to leave, I saw it along the wall: a black, reclining Buddha. It was shiny, and I thought maybe it was carved from obsidian. It looked like it was part of the cave wall. On my return visit in 2016, I learned it was actually made of concrete and painted black. I then stopped and looked around. I saw three orange-robed Buddhist monks looking at me with surprise and alarm.

I stopped, knelt down, and took off my boots. I then went to the altar, grabbed three unlit sticks of incense, lit them from a candle, and held them in my palms as I said the Sanskrit prayer I had learned in Bangkok from the Teacher. When finished I placed the incense in the incense holder, turned and smiled at them, with my hands clasped. They smiled and did the same. They spoke no English and I did not speak any Vietnamese beyond the phrase, "Dow we dow?" which means, I was told, "Where do you hurt?" We looked at each other for a while smiling, then I turned, grabbed my boots, and walked out of the cave to the beach. I put my boots on and wandered a bit further down the beach.

I soon came upon two of my buddies who were arguing with a Vietnamese local. They had no idea what he was saying, but he was definitely complaining about something. The farmer spoke some pidgin English and after a while, I was able to ascertain that my two friends had helped themselves to some ripe bananas from a nearby tree, and that tree belonged to this farmer, and he wanted them to pay for eating his crop. I explained this to my pals and they readily coughed up some piasters (technically, Dong, but nobody wanted to say that word). The farmer smiled and went his way.

We walked back to the chopper and the AC seemed ready to head back, so we did. This was the second great experience I had in Vietnam, the first being that white Buddha statue I saw on top of a mountain in the highlands on my way back from

Nha Trang. These would be the only two nice memories I have of Vietnam over my twenty-seven, give or take, months there.

63 RUNNING ON ADRENALINE

IN CHU LAI ONE DAY WE GOT A call from a unit asking for a pickup. The wounds were gunshot and shrapnel. There were three wounded and two needed litters. We always carried three litters, so that was no problem.

However, the LZ was not secure. We called for Cobra backup and couldn't get anyone. It was also negative for fixed wing, and artillery was busy firing elsewhere. There was artillery active in the area, but they were committed. In fact, the pilot had to map our flight path around the flow of outgoing artillery.

It was a long flight; they were really out in the sticks. We arrived late in the afternoon. They popped smoke and we came in to their LZ, a flat area in short grass. When we landed, I saw six guys come running toward us. They all wore tiger stripe fatigues, LRRPs (Long Range Recon Patrol, pronounced "lerps,") I imagined. They ran and hopped in. One tapped me on the shoulder and said, "Let's go." I asked about the litters, which were right there ready to go, and he said, "That would be for me and my buddy here," pointing to another GI. I laid out the litters, then went about cutting off their pant legs. They were bloody and cutting them was the quickest way to access the wounds. One GI had a gunshot wound to the forearm, no problem. The other two had been hit in their femurs. Not good.

I cut the pant leg off the guy I had spoken with, who ended up being the NCOIC (Non- Commissioned Officer in charge) for the group. His leg was a mess. He was not bleeding much and he was coherent, but his thigh bone had been splintered and part of it was sticking out of his leg. It was so odd looking. Hospitals fix these kinds of problems. All I could do was first aid to keep them from dying on the way to the hospital. I did what I could, and gave him some morphine and tagged him.

I now turned my attention to the other GI and his leg wound. He had been shot in the ankle as well as the thigh, and his foot hung loosely to one side. The tip of the upper part of his ankle wound was caked in mud and grass. It was then I realized that these two had run on these legs. They hadn't wobbled or limped or anything—they ran.

I would add that we took fire on the way out. Later, the Crew Chief found one bullet went through the AC's door and hit his sliding bullet protector on the left side of the chopper.

If the protector hadn't stopped the bullet, it would have hit him in the left shoulder. The other bullet went through the tail but missed the hydraulics and the tail rotor axle.

64 THE SMALLEST "SECURE LZ" I EVER SAW

ONE EVENING, NEAR DUSK, WE RECEIVED A CALL at Chu Lai Dustoff for a pickup. They didn't say much, just gave us coordinates. As we headed out their way, the pilot requested information of the nature of the wounds and whether the LZ was secure. "Shrapnel" and "yes, LZ is secure" were the replies. We searched a while, then found the strobe light marking the LZ as the last of the sunset disappeared over the horizon.

In we came, into tall grass, with a tree line about 400 yards off. I hopped out and looked around, and two fellas were helped on board. They were Marines. "Marines? Where did they come from?" asked the AC. Marines were further north near the DMZ mostly. I shrugged. I looked behind the chopper and saw a fellow lying prone, with a big gun of some sort pointing away from the chopper. He was lying under the tail of the chopper. He eventually got up and got in too. There were 6 of them in all.

As we took off, I examined the two patients. Both had gunshot wounds, one to the leg, and one to the side. Gunshot wounds meant there were folks with guns nearby; shrapnel wounds usually indicate passive enemy action. Had we known there were VC, or NVA nearby, we could have requested gunship cover. I guess the Marines figured that we would not have come if we had known there was a "hot LZ." This turned out to be a problem with units that had never dealt with Dustoff before. They didn't know us from a hole in the ground. I then thought back to the just-completed mission and I realized that the tail of the chopper had been outside the "secure LZ."

65 GUIDED BY A LIGHTER

MARINES NEVER WANT TO TELL YOU ANYTHING. SOMEWHERE outside of Chu Lai we went to get some Marines, again at dusk. Again, the wounds were officially "shrapnel" and the LZ was "secure." It was dead dark outside, no moon. We picked up the strobe light and made our approach. Then the light went off, but we were still in radio contact. "The battery is dead," they said. "Use a flashlight" our AC replied. Then we saw it, and we continued our approach. We were about 100 yards off when it went out. We turned on the landing light and they responded "Turn it off! Turn it off!" so we did. Then we saw a very small flash, similar to a gun firing in the night—but less bright, by far. It was a Bic Lighter. In we came.

This was a larger contingent of Marines, perhaps a company or more. We loaded on 6 fellas and took off, this time with the landing light on, so we could see better the surrounding trees. As we ascended to cruising altitude, the commander on the ground chastised us for using the light and exposing their position.

By this time I had told the AC that all the Marines had gunshot wounds. Our pilot then, in his most acidic voice, asked for the name of the Marine Commander, who refused to give it over the radio. The AC then told him how he would not allow anymore Dustoffs to assist them; we had been unnecessarily lied to, put unnecessarily at risk, and this chopper served more folks then just him and his men. He went on, "Besides, we could have called in Cobras, Spookies, or fast movers (jets doing ground support) for cover . . . let alone artillery. SO FUCK YOU! Over." The Marine officer did not reply.

* * * * * *

Years before, in January 1967, I had hitchhiked from Ottawa, Kansas to Provo, Utah. On my first ride we heard on the radio that three astronauts had died in a fire at Cape Canaveral. My ride let me out near Topeka and on the next few rides, everyone wanted to talk about the astronaut disaster.

I eventually arrived in Colorado and knew I had to stay on US Route 40. It had gotten colder and it seemed the weather was going to change for the worse. One ride dropped me off in Granby, Colorado. I had a small suitcase and I had pasted a cardboard sign on it that said "West." I placed that in front of me and stood there with my thumb out. Soon, the sheriff pulled up, got out, and came over to me. He was very gracious as he said, "Ya know, if you keep holding your thumb out like that, I'm gonna have to put you in jail." I put my thumb down and told him I was headed to Provo to see a friend at BYU.

"Well," he said. "You've got two choices. Wait in my office for two days until the bus arrives, or just walk out of my town." I told him I chose to walk. He cautioned me that "down the road a bit there's a pack of wild dogs. Keep 'n eye out for them." Just then the snow started to come down with a strong wind. I picked up my suitcase and started walking out of town. After ten minutes I turned and could not see a hundred yards back, and there was no sheriff car visible. I decided to stop and hang my thumb at the next vehicle to drive by. None came for an hour, then, finally, one came by and stopped to pick me up. We ended up driving through a blizzard and got hit by an avalanche and then the distributor got wet. But that's another story.

* * * * * *

We had a pickup one night for some gunshot wounds. The LZ was secure when we got there and we loaded one litter patient and two walking wounded. After we took off, I checked everyone out and after re-patching the dressing on the litter patient, I lit up a cigarette and asked him where he was from. "Granby, Colorado," he said. I immediately thought of my adventure there in 1967 and told him the story.

By that time we were approaching the hospital when he grabbed my arm and pulled me close and said, "That sheriff?"

I said, "Yeah?"

"He was my father." Then the medics on the ground pulled him out and I never saw him again. I hope he kept his leg.

66 ORCHIDS

I FIRST BECAME INTERESTED IN ORCHIDS IN JUNIOR high school, back in 1959 or so when the *Philadelphia Bulletin Sunday Edition* ran a two page, full-color spread on orchids. Wow, they were gorgeous! I was hooked. I wanted to find out everything there was about orchids: where they grew, how many kinds there were, why their flowers were so intricate and of many different shapes (unlike roses… boring), how did you grow them and, ultimately, were there any orchids growers nearby I could talk with? I spent a long time getting these answers, but I found out rather quickly there was a Delaware Orchid Society. I found out the meeting time and had my dad drive me there.

I made friends with the members, became one myself, and by the end of that summer the members had given me about 75 plants! They thrived on my back patio, but I had no plan for the winter. I put them in the garage and researched how to grow them. I came up with florescent lights, a self-made humidifier, and confiscated my dad's work bench. I then wrapped the whole thing in a sheet of plastic, and the plants started doing better.

By the time I went to Fork Union, I had taught Dad how to care for them. (They are tough plants. It's harder to kill them than to flower them). A year later I was off to college and three semesters later, I'd flunked out and was being drafted.

So in late August 1969, I planned one of my seven day R&Rs to be in Sydney, Australia, to coincide with the 6th World Orchid Conference there. I went by Air Vietnam from Saigon to Bangkok, then Malaysian Airlines to Singapore, then Qantas to Sydney via Darwin on a standard civilian flight.

On the flight to Darwin, I was the only soldier. They asked all of us if we had any mud on our shoes or boots. (They wanted to keep out anthrax). During those conversations a stewardess learned that I was a US soldier serving in Vietnam. She apparently made some arrangements because on the flight from Darwin to Sydney I was presented with a voucher from Qantas Airlines to pay for my hotel stay in Sydney! I was amazed.

At the hotel, I walked into my room, got undressed, looked at the bathtub, then f lushed the toilet to see if it actually rotated in the opposite direction of toilets in the northern hemisphere. I realized that was not a good test, so I filled the sink and let it drain and watched the little water tornado form. Gosh! It did go in the opposite direction! Cool. Let's hear it for physics!

All this while, the tub was filling with very warm water. I got in, settled in till the water was just at my nose, and fell asleep. I woke up four hours later. The water was cool. It was also dark red like wine. Curious. I got out, dried off, then looked in the mirror to shave and saw a distinctive line from the bottom of my chin going back to my ears. Below that line I was a tanned white, above the line I was a dark tan. A year's worth of laterite (the tropical soil, rich in iron and aluminum) had leached out of my skin during my soak. It took a while but I finally made myself presentable.

I went downstairs and ran into Ed Arndt, a member of the Delaware Orchid Society who had helped me with orchids back in junior high and high school. He invited me to eat supper with his group so I did. I only remember two things from that meal. First was that Mr. Arndt ordered a claret wine, something I had never heard of before. The other was the baby carrots they served. They were tiny! I had never seen such small carrots, and I didn't expect much from them when I bit into one. I was wrong. It was sweet, and just a little crunchy ("al dente" is a word I learned later in life). My life's opinion of carrots had changed then and there.

I want to say this about Mr. Arndt. He was a CPA by trade, but a real gentleman, an innovative orchid grower who knew how to get things done for pennies. I often invited myself over to see his greenhouse and he was always gracious and informative. I learned a lot about orchids from him. I also learned that he was proud that his name was "one of only a few" that had four consonants in a row. I miss him.

I knew I wanted to see some of the Conference, but it was mostly pretty dry "talk" with too many charts. The orchid show was great, but after that I spent most of my time going from bar to bar checking out Australians, their bars, their cider bars, and their women. There were three women for every GI in that part of town where the GI bars were. The women flocked there, I learned later, because the Australian men didn't treat their women the way Americans did. I recall one conversation where after a while the girl asked me if I was in the US Navy. "No, I'm in the Army," I replied. "Oh, but you're such a gentleman. I thought you were a Navy spunk." While I was wondering what a "spunk" was, she turned and walked away. At this point I was still "in love" with Kathy, even though she had dumped me.

I left that bar and visited a cider house. I was amazed, they actually served cider, in bottles! I had a few then realized it was hard cider, but it had no alcohol scent. Being woozy reminded me of my three-day death dance so I stopped and left the bar to take a walk. Just outside three women started asking me for directions.

I told them "I'm new here" and then asked them about their accent. "We're Lithuanian," they replied. We talked a while, and I said something about how I was glad they were on this side of the Iron Curtain. At that point one of the three asked me if I wanted to go back to their place and smoke some weed, have some beers, and party. I was still anxious to walk off my buzz and I thanked them then declined. As I walked away, I realized they wanted to have sex, or so I thought, so I turned and looked for them, but they were gone. Idiot!

I ended up walking all over Sydney. I came to some university, wandered in, and asked about applications. The lady said I could take classes "Once you have matriculated." I replied, "Oh, okay. Thanks." As I walked out, I wondered what "matriculated" meant.

I continued walking. I went down to the harbor and saw the new opera house under construction. It was beautiful and uniquely designed. I ended up walking most of the night. It was during this walk that I came to the conclusion that being "in love" was a mental disease and had nothing to do with "love." "Love" was hard, "in love" was just wanting the next new thing. By 4 AM I had wandered into a residential part of town that was absolutely dead quiet. Not even a taxi. By 6 AM I was back at my hotel and I slept all that day until the next morning.

I was in Sydney six nights and seven days in all. I returned on Qantas as well, again via Darwin. From Darwin it was a night flight. Midway into the flight I noticed out my left window that there was a lot of lightening happening. With each lightning f lash I was able to get a partial picture of the view. I guessed we were at 30,000 feet and the thunderheads were a lot higher than we were. All was clear below. Then one flash followed another is quick succession. It was then that I saw the outline of the Gulf of Tomini by strobe light. I could tell by its shape. Though I didn't know the gulf's name, I knew the island that surrounded it was Sulawesi, east of Borneo. Cool. One of my Life Goals had been to go to Borneo and I'd achieved it and was now viewing it from the sky.

67 FLYING WITH THE 54TH

WHILE I WAS AT THE 54TH IN CHU Lai we hauled a lot of patients—and a lot of KIAs. The unit was a remarkable one. The year before, the Detachment's XO (Executive Officer), Maj. Patrick Brady, earned the Medal of Honor for evacuations he piloted. A total of three Medals of Honor were awarded to Dustoff personnel during the war. Major Brady was the first.

During one ten-month period, the unit only had three flyable choppers, yet during that time they hauled 21,435 patients. Sixteen months before I arrived, all six of their choppers had been shot down while supporting an ARVN operation. They borrowed a chopper and lost that one too. It was an extremely hostile area.

It remained a busy place when I arrived. I don't have any numbers on how many choppers and crews were lost, but it was a few. I recalled Randy "Rotorblades" Radigan's comments about wanting to be around to show the new pilots the details of the terrain. It seemed to me most of our pilots in the 54th were fairly new to the unit. I wasn't assigned a crew chief.

Medics rotated for a few days, then a day off.

Down south there were no Marines, but up here there were plenty. There also seemed to be more SOCOM (Special Operations Command) teams, Green Berets, and LRRP's (Long Range Recon Patrols), plus the 101st Airborne. However, the main unit we served was the American (23rd) Division.

The American Division has an unusual history. It was formed from "orphan" regiments from other National Guard divisions during the growth of the US Army at the beginnings of WWII. For some reason, National Guard (NG) divisions had four regiments while "regular Army" divisions have three. Each NG division shed one regiment and three of these orphans were sent as a "task force" to New Caledonia in 1942. Later these orphans were made into the American. It was called the American,

New Caledonia Division and the name was shortened to the "American" Division. Most US Divisions have a number; this one didn't until after WWII when it was designated the 23rd Infantry Division. But the American name was already in use and it stuck.

In 1942, the 164th Infantry Regiment of the Americal fought alongside the 1st Marine Division on Guadalcanal and became the first US Army unit to conduct offensive operations in WWII. The Americal last fought in the Philippines and participated in the occupation of Japan post war until late 1945, when it was deactivated. It was reactivated for two years in 1954 and was spread out across islands in the Caribbean and Panama. It was reactivated a third time on September 25, 1967 at Chu Lai in Vietnam from Task Force Oregon, composed of the 1st Brigade of the 101st Airborne, the 3rd brigade of the 25th Infantry Division, and the 196th Light Infantry Brigade, plus support units. All these brigades were deployed separately in 1966 to Vietnam. So the new Americal Division did not have a cohesive recent history that created camaraderie and pride in the unit. It was related, in name only, to the Division's gallant history of WWII.

Everyone I had met in 'Nam who was part of a frontline combat force was proud of their unit. The 1st Infantry Division was called the "Worst Infantry Division" and the "Big Dead One" by members of the 101st Division, and the "Big Red One" called the "Screaming Eagles" the "Hundred and Worst," "One-O-Worst" and the "Puking Pigeons."

The 4th Inf. Division—in a play on words of the Roman Numeral "IV"—was called "Ivy" or "Poison Ivy."

The 9th Inf. Div. was often called by others as the "psychedelic cookie" division, and the 25th Inf. Div. called the "electric strawberry" division because of their patches. These names were all used in jest, but nobody ever referred to the 23rd Infantry Division as anything but the Americal Division.

There was also the 1st Cavalry Division (Airmobile). It was reconfigured once from horses to armor, then this last time from armor into the first helicopter mobile unit. It was usually referred to as "the 1st Air Cav" or "Blackhorse." Guys from other units called them the "Worst Air Cav," but never to their faces. I was told that in the Korean War, this unit performed badly and the commanding general changed their patch (see Figure below) to show the road they never captured on the horse they never rode, and the yellow speaks for itself. But this is simply a false rumor. I later found out that this is actually their original patch from the 1920s. The yellow is the sunshine of Texas, where the unit was formed; the horse head shows the unit's heritage as cavalry; the black denotes iron and a change to armored vehicles; the stripe denotes the belt worn by soldiers to carry a scabbard for a sword; and the shield shape signifies their purpose in battle. Yellow is also the traditional color of cavalry.

I also found out that their tragedy in Korea was not of their making. They were the first unit to be attacked by the Chinese Red Army up by the Yellow River. They were outnumbered and outgunned. They got caught in a trap but some escaped. History buffs should Google "Battle of Usan" for more. I think they acquitted themselves admirably.

The 1st Air Cav is one of the most highly decorated units in the US military. And they certainly proved their mettle in their first battle in Vietnam where they relieved the siege of Plei Me close to Plei Ku. They pursued the retreating NVA until the NVA made a stand in the Ia Drang and lost. This battle is memorialized

1st Air Cav shoulder patch

1st Air Cav shoulder patch

in the book *We Were Soldiers Once and Young*, written by Lt. Gen. Hal Moore and Joseph Galloway, the latter who I met in 1997 in Lawrence, Kansas, on his way to Colorado. His book is the basis for the movie *We Were Soldiers*, which everyone should see. The commander who led the 1st Battalion, 7th Cavalry Regiment of the 1st Cav there, Lt. Col. Hal Moore, died on February 10, 2017, while I was writing this memoir, as a Lt. General (Ret.). This successful battle earned them the Presidential Unit Citation, the first in the Vietnam War.

I have no idea how many Marine units were in Vietnam. I know the 1st Marine Division, the one that saved Guadalcanal in WWII with part of the Americal Division, was there and at least part of the 3rd Marine Division as well. There were a bunch of Marine battalions and brigades in I Corps, and whether they were part of the 1st or 3rd division or detached units I cannot say.

The units in I Corps consisted of Marines, 1st Air Cav, 101st Airborne Division, and the Americal at the division level. There were also Long Range Recon Patrols, Special Forces, MIKE Forces (Mobile Strike Forces formed of Montagnards and Cambodian irregulars and organized by the Special Forces), detached American and Korean brigades, and ARVN units that had proved themselves in the defense of Hue and other locales during Tet 1968. All of these units were hardened by Tet, and the infiltration and fighting in I Corps didn't let up after the Tet offensive ended in August 1968. Down south there were more VC and some NVA (North Vietnamese

Army) near the Cambodian border, but up north, the VC seemed more disciplined and the NVA were much more plentiful.

The NVA attempted to capture Da Nang during Tet (February 1968). They were fiercely repulsed by the Koreans, the 1st Marine Division, and the Americal. The NVA "disappeared" after they withdrew and reformed near Kham Duc and assaulted it on May 10–12, 1968. Only a light Americal unit was present and they managed to hold off the attack until everyone could be withdrawn. An unknown number of Nung (Montagnard) and ARVN (Army of Vietnam) soldiers, along with thirteen US Military (Army and Marine) were killed and ninety-one wounded, plus nine U.S. military aircraft had been shot down, including two C-130s. I don't know if there were any Air Force losses. I call it a successful battling withdrawal; others call it a defeat. Take your pick. But it affected the morale of the entire Americal thereafter.

68 SHRAPNEL OR GUNSHOT? NOT JUST SEMANTICS

BY THE TIME I ARRIVED IN CHU LAI, a year of flying Dustoff had passed but the fighting had not declined much. Like I said, we hauled a lot of wounded and a lot of KIAs were thrown in with them. The fighting units up north had a different attitude about Dustoff pickups than down south in III Corps. Army units up north treated Dustoff as they did down south, but non-Army units seemed unsure of us. All I know for sure is that the non-Army units often told us the wounded we're coming to pick up were "shrapnel" injuries when, in fact, they were gunshot wounds. I guess they really didn't interact with us much since, I guessed, Marines had Navy rescue choppers mostly.

It seemed these non-Army units were smaller in the field here in I Corps, and when they took wounded, a higher percentage of their fighting capability became incapacitated. This made evacuation of the KIAs tactically necessary so the unit could keep all its remaining people fighting. Down south there were a few instances where we took out KIAs during ongoing battles in the woods, but in the more open areas supply choppers hauled out the KIAs after unloading. This didn't happen as much up north due to the mountainous, treed terrain where hovering was often the only way to load or unload.

When fighting the enemy on the ground and your men take hits, the commander needs to make tactical decisions about how many men to divert from fighting to stretcher duty. Dustoffs require a landing zone, or a hover zone, and the terrain in I Corps is less accommodating sometimes. So you're fighting and faced with a decision to remove some men from fighting to take care of the wounded and dead, or you need to move your unit to a place where the chopper can land. These are difficult decisions to make while you're actively returning fire at an enemy only 25 yards away.

The Dustoff pilot needs the most accurate information possible in order to pick up as many wounded as possible, while the commander on the ground needs to ensure the safety of his remaining men while still fighting. It's difficult all around. And it explains, for me, why we were lied to or misled by the men on the ground as to the true nature of the situation: they didn't want us to go away without picking up their wounded and dead, so they almost always downplayed the true situation. Especially the LRRPs and the Marines.

We got a call to come pick up two wounded Marines. "Shrapnel" we were told. Our crew decided they were probably gunshot wounds and were prepared for that. By the time we got there, there were seven wounded—all gunshots. We loaded them on, took hits on the ground and during take-off. We returned fire, as did some of the Marines we loaded on.

As with other small units in battle, these wounded weren't on litters. Once out of range, I opened litters and placed the two worst on them and went to work. I had looked over the patients and identified two who were not going to make it without heroic efforts. The others my crew chief handed bandages to so they could patch themselves while I went to work. Both of the critical patients were gut shot. Only one had a larger exit wound, the other had no exit wound. So I worked on him first. After opening him with my scalpel for a better view, I clamped as many bleeding vessels as I could locate. I gave an IV (he needed a second IV before we got him back) and checked his other wounds.

Convinced I had done all I could, I went to the other one. His exit wound was massive; almost half of his back on one side was missing or in pieces. I clamped what I could until I ran out of clamps. I needed more clamps. I grabbed some of the other Marines and told them to "pinch here." Three Marines, five pinches. Good. I put an IV in him and opened it up full throttle. I thought he was going to make it but the blood loss was great. I checked the first Marine again and put in the second IV and slowed it down, checked the bleeding and had the Marine with the one free hand apply pressure on the stubborn bleeder.

We were on approach to the hospital while I was checking the second gut-shot Marine. I saw that he was bleeding clear fluid, which meant he'd lost all his own blood and was bleeding the IV fluid. I checked his Dog Tag and told the AC to tell the hospital to be sure to have three pints of O Negative blood ready to infuse before he was removed from the chopper. When we landed, the blood was not there. As we off loaded them onto stretchers, a physician came running out and replaced my IV with the blood. The doc was squeezing the cold blood into the Marine— no time to warm it up—as they wheeled him away. He died in ER a few moments later.

We went back to our LZ and I tried to clean the chopper. That Marine had bled out in the chopper and all that blood had managed to get everywhere. My Delaware flag was soaked again.

I found a short piece of rib bone and what I think was a piece of lung in the chopper. It took five one-gallon cans of water and a half gallon of hydrogen peroxide to get the chopper back to "acceptable."

There were other missions just like this one and I'm just not going to write them down. One retelling is enough. But I will add that once I returned to the States and was met with the derision and abuse given to us Vietnam Veterans, my thoughts go back to memories like these where my actions made a difference, sometimes, even if the "civilians" don't fricking understand, or care.

69 ELEPHANT ATTACK

ONE UNUSUAL MISSION WE HAD WAS WHEN SOME LRRPs called and requested a pick up. When we asked the nature of the wound they replied, "elephant attack." Never heard that one before. They were in a dicey area. In fact, they were there to observe and report enemy troop movements. I never learned what they did. (The one time I asked, the GI said he'd have to kill me if he told me. "Should I go on?" he asked.)

Their position required that they drag the wounded one about two klicks (kilometers) east for pickup. During that time we were en route, we used the radio transponder to keep track of them until they felt clear. They didn't want to use smoke so we tried reflections off of their knife. That was iffy but we got a bead finally and came in and landed. I brought out the litter, opened it, and they placed their buddy on it. Once in and with good altitude, I checked him out. It looked like his leg where it meets the pelvis had been stretched so that the thigh bone was no longer in the hip socket. The entire area was blue with bruises. I saw no edema, an indication of internal bleeding, and wasn't convinced he had any broken bones. He was alert, and the color of his fingernails and lips was good. Blood flow looked good; no shock.

We had a ways back to the hospital so I asked what happened. They told me they were in their concealed position when a baby elephant walked in between them. Everyone remained still hoping it would leave, but it started nosing one of them. It cried and then the mother arrived. She went into full mother mode and trampled, getting this one fellow square on the hip.

After unloading their clips, they ran, then realized one of their men was still on the ground. They reloaded and charged the mother, who departed with her calf. Then they got on the horn, called us, and started dragging him to a more secure area. They were lucky their target didn't respond and come looking for them once they opened fire on the mother elephant.

We dropped them off then returned to our Dustoff LZ.

70 BENT SKIDS

THE NEXT NIGHT WE GOT A CALL FROM some Marines for two gunshot wounds. The AC remembered the call sign and told us it was that same Marine unit that lied to us before about "shrapnel" wounds. The AC thanked him for being up front and said our ETA would be about 25 minutes. It was dark and there was no moon. But we knew the area and flew by the landmarks we could make out, then went on instruments once all the lights were behind us.

Hueys have this neat panel instrument that shows the direction of the radio signal you are communicating with. It's a direction finder. Once you pass over it, the dial goes all the way to one side. You turn and realign the dial and select your landing spot. In theory.

The Marines did not want to use a light to mark their position, so we used this direction finder. We had come over the spot and made a turn, but the ground was hilly and we thought there were trees in the area. The AC then switched on the landing light for a moment, ruining our night vision, then switched it off, then came in for the landing. We all noticed that the ground was way too close and we hit the ground hard. I looked out my side and saw our left skid sticking almost straight out sideways. The crew chief confirmed the same on the right.

The AC grabbed the collective and gained altitude and told the Marines this mission was aborted and we would send in another Dustoff to complete the mission. Once we had gained altitude, the AC radioed Chu Lai airfield and told them our situation. After two minutes they came back and told us to circle at one end of the airstrip until fifteen minutes after the 20-minute fuel warning light comes on. That way if we caught fire there wouldn't be a lot of fuel to add to the fire. So we circled. We had used almost an hour in fuel already so we had another two hours or so before the light would come on.

We discussed our plans for the landing. We were to land on a large sand pile they were constructing as we spoke. It was decided that first, the AC would come into a hover, and let the crew and the co-pilot get out. Once we were clear he would then land the chopper on the sand pile, hopefully keeping it upright the whole time. The real problem would come once the blades were no longer providing lift and some gyroscopic stability—the chopper could roll over and then the blades would come off. It's a total commit once the turbine was off.

After that, it was two hours of chit chat and listening to Armed Forces Radio tunes until the 20-minute warning light came on. After fifteen minutes, we slowly hovered down to a near landing on the sand. The crew chief and I got out and opened the doors for the AC and co-pilot. We then pulled back the chicken plates so they could exit. The co-pilot exited and the three of us moved to a safe distance, the AC landed the chopper on the sand and turned off the engine. We waited until the blades stopped, which takes a while—maybe three or four minutes. But the chopper did not tip over. We got back to our unit's RTO and discovered we were all grounded until incident statements were made. Within three days we were all flying again.

71   TUNNEL TOURS

WHEN WE GOT CALLS FOR MISSIONS, WE ALWAYS tried to ascertain the nature of the wounds and the nature of the LZ. We got a call about 2AM one morning about a guy in the field with a fever. We were told it "wasn't life threatening" and so we told them we would do the pick up at first light. When the time came, we took off and headed almost due west, into the mountains.

The AC got off the horn with everyone he needed to talk to in order to find a clear path, and figured out that between the artillery, the air strikes, and the B52 runs, there was no way we could get to the location *right now*.

We saw a fire base nearby on top of one of the mountains we were flying by and we settled down there to wait. The AC confirmed it was going to be at least two hours before firing stopped. Their guns were firing and were part of the reason we could not proceed. So I started familiarizing myself with an artillery firebase.

While walking around I saw a small, homemade sign that said, "VC tunnel tours 25¢." I asked someone who walked by what that was about. He said, "Oh, we discovered a VC tunnel complex under our base. I guess the VC figured it was the last place we'd shell." I asked if it was okay to check out and he assured me it was. "There's a candle, just light it and go on in." In I went.

The tunnel was about five feet high, so I had to stoop to enter. It was also just barely wide enough for me to make my way without turning sideways. I walked a ways and found a little cubbyhole halfway up from the floor. There was the candle. I lit it and continued. I hit a slope going down and stopped. I could hear the muffled sound of the guns up top blazing away and tried to feel if there was any vibration. None.

After going in about 100 feet, I discovered I'm not comfortable in tight spaces and decided to retreat. I passed the candle I had lit and blew it out and continued up the path. I emerged to sunlight and fresh air and felt better. I remembered the human blood-bank patients I had treated and thought about their two years in the tunnels, being fed rice soup and wondering about the future while being bled dry by their enemy. I shuddered, but I have never been able to forget about those blood-bank prisoners we helped rescue.

I went back to our chopper and gave our crew the lowdown on the tunnels. Then the guns went silent and someone came over and told our AC that we were clear to go ahead. We were able to pick up the fever patient as well as two gunshot wounds and three KIAs from a small unit probably doing a recon.

72 MY BREAKING POINT

THE WHOLE AFTERNOON AND EVENING WAS SPENT PICKING up more wounded. Most were gunshot wounds. All the units we responded to seemed to be small units that had no time to be worrying about wounded or KIAs while they continued their fighting with Charlie. Some of the pickups required we request gunships for cover. All the LZs were *hot*.

We carried a lot of dead GIs. I didn't realize it at the time, but I had become deadened inside. Years later I began to understand that by not caring, I was avoiding the pain. But that day, I felt no pain, just anger.

The last pickup had one gunshot and seven KIAs. I remained agitated. I patched him up as best I could and gave an IV, but he was bleeding profusely. I clamped where I could, but it was a deep wound in his leg with a large exit hole. It was close to his hip, and a tourniquet wasn't effective. I put the flashlight in my mouth and dug into the wound with both hands, one loaded with another clamp. I found a bleeder and clamped it, but it started bleeding somewhere else. I put my thumb on it and told the AC we'd need a surgeon present when we offload to help stop the bleeding. I looked around, trying to figure out what else I could do. No ideas. Pressure, keep the pressure up, check the IV level . . . pressure.

When we landed, a surgeon was there. He climbed in and assisted, then once upto-speed, took over. Two medics with him had brought lights so the surgeon could see clearly. The other hospital medics—all FNGs—stood around, wondering what to do. I signaled for them to come over and offload the KIAs. They came, but were repulsed by what they saw of what was left of the KIAs. I snapped. I grabbed one of the dead and dragged him out and let him drop onto the ground. Then I did another the same way. Then another. I finally told the medics standing around to "Get goin!" and had them unload the rest of the dead. Suddenly I realized I had crossed a line. The three

GIs I had unloaded I'd treated like logs, not heroes. I was ashamed of myself. Then the doctor got out and shook his head. Not one we'd brought back that trip was alive. Death, death, death.

No one said anything to me on the way back to our Dustoff LZ. There were no more missions that night and after cleaning the chopper and changing my clothes, I tried to sleep in the RTO. I didn't get a wink.

After realizing I was burned out as a Dustoff medic, I went to the Flight Surgeon and told him about the ringing in my ears and the balance issues I had. I had kept these secret after the IED explosion at Nui Ba Din on February 2 1969, when our chopper was damaged by an IED. I had talked with one co-pilot in Lai Khe about it at the time and he suggested that if I didn't tell anyone I could keep my wings and everything would go on as usual.

Now realizing I was emotionally dead or worse, I knew my new "don't give a shit" attitude was a danger to the rest of the crew. They needed someone who was 100 percent, not 99 percent. I owed it to them to give up my wings. So I did. The Flight Surgeon revoked my flight status. I was transferred three days later.

73 NEW ORDERS: 91ST EVAC

MY TRANSFER ORDERS SENT ME TO THE 91ST Evacuation Hospital there at Chu Lai. I was a Spec 5, with over two years in-country and fifteen months as a Dustoff medic. They figured I had seen it all so they put me in charge of the Pre-Op ward. I was officially, NCOIC Pre-Op. I noticed right away that we were on twelve-hour shifts. I wondered why since we had our full complement of staff. Within two days I had my answer: almost a third of the enlisted men were non-functional due to drug addiction.

On the day I arrived, I went to my new hooch. It was a two-story wooden building. Stairs on the outside led up to the second floor. Inside, two enterprising Sp4s down at the other end had constructed a wall, making their sleeping area semi-private. They'd run out of stolen wood, so when someone was in the top bunk, I could see half their body. They'd even put a door on their "room." Not one of those four guys ever reported for duty. They just smoked opium, pot, and perhaps other stuff. I never spoke to them.

About a week after I arrived, the Colonel who ran the hospital marched in. I had the night shift so there I was in bed, recognized him, and got up at attention and said, "Officer on deck!" He ignored me and walked down to the new room. He could see the person he wanted over the top on the top rack of the bunk bed. The Colonel stopped and looked at the guy, who was reading a comic book. The Colonel said, "Are you going on shift today like we talked about?" The guy put down the comic book, looked at the Colonel and gave him the finger, then went back to his comic. The Colonel stood there flummoxed, then turned and marched right out of the hooch.

I spoke about this later with a Master Sergeant and asked him what the hell was going on? How come the Colonel didn't have that guy put in the stockade? The MSgt. said, "The Colonel's new, he's only been in command a few weeks and he's just discovered why we're on 12-hour shifts."

I asked, "Is he going to report it?" The MSgt. Said, "Probably not." "Why not?" I asked.

"If he reports it, the Army will look at all their paperwork and say, 'Well, this is new, this must have happened on your watch', which will look bad for the Colonel. No more promotions."

I realized the Army had created a reward system through which bad news did not travel upwards to the ears of someone who could rectify the problem. I felt bad about that, and it started to feed some other questions I had about the war.

So, here I was, in charge of the Pre-Op ward. The Docs and Nurses gave me a thorough review of the ward, the tools available, and told me what they expected from me. They prepared me well, I think. I had an assistant, but as time went by, he showed up less and less. I reported his absences every day.

Like with Dustoff, the work tended to come in droves. A battle would rage somewhere and the wounded would flood in. We would be busy for six to twenty hours, then things would die down, with just local accident emergencies of the everyday sort.

We once had a patient brought in who was diagnosed with pneumonic plague, which is highly contagious. As soon as the docs realized that, they called the Dustoff unit that brought him to have the crew quarantined. They also ordered to destroy the helicopter. That was all done, but the only one who died was the Vietnamese civilian brought in with the plague.

74 DRAGONFLIES AND DEBRIDING

WHEN THINGS WERE DULL I HUNG OUT IN the ER where everyone else was. I was mostly by myself in the Pre-Op. Every day I spent two hours sterilizing every surface in the room with Betadine and a mop dedicated for that purpose. I always swept first, then mopped, then wiped. One day I was sweeping and found a two-foot long bright green snake. After capture the physician on duty called it a green pit viper. None of us knew how deadly the bite was, but we did get rid of it. Someone called it a "two stepper," meaning that you've got two steps after it bites you until you're dead. I'm not sure that's true. In all my time as a medic in Vietnam, I had seen only one snake bite patient, and he turned out to be faking it.

I was on the night shift, so my shift began at 6 PM. We were right on the coast, atop a cliff that overlooked the South China Sea. At night the ER was lit with florescent lights, and the doors were swung wide open leading to both the helipad LZ and to the ambulance driveway.

This allowed our lights—*flickering* lights to insects—to attract dragonflies in the evenings right around sunset. I didn't learn till later that certain dragonflies are *crepuscular*, flying at dawn and sunset, looking for prey that come out at sunset and retire at daybreak, like mosquitoes.

Some dragonflies flew into our ER and just never left. I made it my job to collect them since a neighbor friend of Dad's was an entomologist. I decided to make a collection and send them to him. These dragonflies were magnificent. They were very large, the largest I have ever seen, and brightly colored, with many different colors. (I have since learned that these were members of the *Libellulidae* family of dragonflies, the largest in the world). Some were copper colored, others were metallic green or blue, and one was chalk white. I saved the best specimens, pinned them, and put them in a box and mailed them to my dad's friend. The rest I just nabbed, took outside, and released. Off they went. This happened every night until the monsoon arrived in December.

The routine in the Pre-Op ward was pretty normal. Patients were sorted in the ER. Those requiring surgery went directly to surgery. Others were patched up and returned to duty, and others were sent to me. The ones that came in to see me were of two sorts: those who needed some stitches and debriding (the removal of necrotic or dead tissue), and those that were not emergencies but needed some kind of care or patching, or preparation before they went to surgery, like shaving the area around the wound.

One physician took me under his wing. He would wheel in a patient, then explain to me what needed to be done. We had two surgical tables, lots of surgical lights, and all the surgical tools needed were sterilized. We had a place to wash up and "scrub," and all the other medical paraphernalia needed to perform surgery.

We would examine the wound(s), look at x-rays to show there was no shrapnel, or if there was, where it was located. It was at this time that I learned that glass does not show up in x-rays. Then he'd explain what I should do and what to look for when debriding and sewing up the wounds. He watched me stitch patients and then showed me how to make the stitches so they would not leave scars. We talked about preferred stitching needles for different situations, preferred sewing threads, and different types of stitches for different situations.

Within two weeks I felt well-prepared. One day we got a patient who had been roofing when the pile of galvanized steel roofing began to slide down the roof. One sheet took off and slid all the way down, and caught this soldier on the ground in the forehead. When he was wheeled in, unconscious, I saw that his scalp was flipped back and his skull exposed. His scalp was still attached in the back of his head. The Doc wheeled him in, looked at me, and asked me, "Are you good?"

"Yes," I replied, and I took over. I scrubbed, gloved, and set up a sterile field. I cleaned and shaved his scalp where needed, then injected Lidocaine where I needed to debride the wound. The patient was out, but I didn't want him coming to and yelling about the pain. After the wound was cleaned, I considered the task of sewing his scalp back onto his skull. The Doc had shown me that you need to plan your sewing. You don't want to end up with some "extra" skin on one side and short on the other side. I flipped the scalp back over the skull and put in a stitch in the middle, just above his forehead. I looked at the skin remaining on either side and once convinced I had the scalp placed right, I did the stitch. Then, half way from that stitch to where the tear ended, on either side, I put in another stitch. Here, the scalp was well fitted, then I completed the stitching using the lock-stitch. In all, it took several hours to make those 104 stitches—the most I'd ever used on a single wound. Two weeks later, that guy walked into my ward and thanked me. That was great.

75 LEFT TO DIE AT CHU LAI

ONE NIGHT WE HAD A MASS CAUSALITY SITUATION that lasted about five hours. This one GI was brought in with massive head wounds. Head wounds are not "emergencies" in a war zone. In the time it would take to, possibly, save this one guy, the docs could have saved the lives of 15 or 20 others. So the kid and litter were wheeled over to the side.

Hours later, after all the commotion of the night's battle subsided, I called the doc's attention to the fellow with the head wound. The doc came over, examined him, and decided there was little he could do. "The kid's gone," he said. "If he ever woke up, he wouldn't know who he was, would be incontinent, and probably would never speak. He's gone, let him die." I rolled him over to a corner of the emergency room, drew a drape, and stood beside him. He was still in the uniform he'd put on a few days before, I supposed, by the look of it.

The shift ended but I stayed with him. I wondered about his family, his mom and dad. Did he have any brothers or sisters? A Girlfriend? A favorite teacher? A pet dog? Had he ever had sex? I hoped he had. Then I started thinking about the "meaning" of his death. Was he just in the wrong place at the wrong time, or had he died while saving someone else's life? I started feeling bad again about how I had treated those KIAs on my last mission and I decided that this man would have some dignity in his death. I wondered if he could hear. I tried to speak but there were no words.

He died about 10 o'clock in the morning; but he didn't die alone.

76 BETRAYED

THE MONSOON CAME THAT DECEMBER, AT LEAST THAT'S what I called it. There was a drizzling rain that continued for nineteen days straight. The rain never got faster, nor did it ever slow down. It just rained continually. And every day it got a little chillier. We were only issued a cot and two sheets. I had won a foam pillow in a poker game and used that every day. The foam was originally light tan but had turned rusty red from all the laterite dust. I sweat in my sleep and with time, the laterite washing off my neck went into the foam.

That pillow became my teddy bear in 'Nam. When I got home, one day my Mom washed it without asking me, and it fell completely apart. I was devastated, until I got a new one the next day. But the new one did smell awfully clean. Too clean.

Back to the rain. I had a sheet to sleep on and a sheet to cover me, which was luxury to anything I'd had before. But it got cooler every day and by day fourteen, I was cold going to bed in the morning. I slept in my clothes, and by the end, I had doubled my top sheet and wore my clothes. Then, the rain stopped, the sun came out, and the cold spell was over.

Just after the end of the monsoon we got word that there would be an official visit by the wife of the President of Vietnam: Mrs. Nguyen Van Thieu. The visit occurred during the daytime, when I was off duty, but I stayed up to watch the pomp and circumstance. There were MPs dressed in their whites, a bunch of top US brass, reporters, and Vietnamese guards and soldiers too. I sat outside my barracks and watched the procession as she went from Ward 1 to Ward 2 to Ward 3. Each visit to a ward took about ten minutes while she, I suppose, shook hands with all the patients. She then entered Ward 3, where our burn patients were. That visit took a little longer. Then she came out, and walked to Ward 5, bypassing Ward 4. I almost threw up.

Ward 4 was where the Vietnamese civilian patients were, and I had just witnessed the wife of their President avoiding seeing them. She was not acting like the wife of the Leader, encouraging her people to "carry on" and giving them hope. I realized she was not one of the Good Guys. At that moment I felt the war was lost.

In one fleeting second, I realized that all the lives lost, all the dreams postponed or ended, all the pain, all the fear and terror suffered by everyone on our side of this war was possibly for nothing. I changed then and there.

Little did I know it, but beginning then, I was coming to realize we, the soldiers, had been betrayed. I saw that we were not fighting to help some people become free, but to support a few rulers who did not give a damn about those they ruled. We had all been had. Nobody believed in this cause we were asked to fight—indeed, had been ordered to fight. There was no noble cause.

77   WELCOME HOME, HIPPIE STYLE

IT WAS A LONG FLIGHT HOME, AND I must have slept most of the way. I remember there were a lot of GIs fresh out of the boonies. They still had the red marks of laterite on their boots and clothes. They were not units of men being transferred home who shared a year in hell together.

They were individuals from many units; they did not know each other, and they had no shared history. They had nothing to talk about with each other, specifically. Unlike WWII, where units rotated home aboard a ship that took weeks to get home, and where you had the opportunity to review your feelings with others who had shared your experiences, we were coming home in a jet, individually, with no decompression time. Everybody was an FNG to everybody else.

I literally kissed the ground when I returned—several of us did. We had a great breakfast: ham, eggs, ham, toast and jelly, ham, fresh juice, and ham. Then there was the usual "hurry-up and wait" as we went through the ritual of separation from active duty.

Top: *Crew Wings, Meritorious Unit Commendation.* Bottom (L to R): *Purple Heart, 15 Air Medals, Good Conduct Medal, Vietnam Service Medal, National Defense Medal, Vietnamese Government Medal for Service, Vietnam Gallantry Cross with Palm Leaf, four Overseas Combat Zone bars. Red Bar: For 45th Medical Company, 1968.*

Several of the pieces of paperwork I was provided consisted of my medals.

Finally, I was in the Seattle airport. I went to the Hertz counter and asked to rent a car. I really wanted to unwind a bit and driving across the country would be a great way to do it. I was 23 years old. I had done what my country asked me to do: kill, save lives, survive. The ladybehind the Hertz counter said I was too young to rent their cars. I had to be 25 years old, since that was the presumed age of assuming "responsibility."

My plans for a nice leisurely drive across the nation evaporated. So, I went with my travel voucher and got a ticket for Philadelphia. I was wearing my dress uniform, since I figured this would help garner some sympathy with stand-by seating. I had already been told by the sergeant at the base, "That uniform, and a dime, will buy you a cuppa coffee."

I went over to an airport cafeteria and got in line. Right behind me a hippie fell into line. I turned and we started a conversation. We talked about little stuff, *where ya from* and all that. At the cashier's desk, I plunked down a $10 bill and paid for both our lunches. We found a table, sat, and I gobbled up the conversation while we ate. Eventually, the conversation turned to what I did, and 'Nam. I told him I was a medic and related a few instances.

Eventually the meal was gone and his flight was called. He got up, looked at me, and said, "You know, it's too bad you weren't killed over there." He turned and left.

In the WWII movies I watched as kid, returning GIs always got a parade, or something, not this. What did I do? I had served my country honorably. I was proud of what I had accomplished. I had done my duty as my father had. *I was a good person!*

I thought about it for a long time, then wrote a poem:

ODE TO A MISGUIDED HIPPIE

When I left 'Nam, I was on a jet; Two hundred and twelve of us, each a Vet. The day before we were all in battle, Tonight we land in old Seattle.

At Sea-Tac it's standby, so I go and eat; I see a hippie and I offer a seat.
We chatted, and rambled, and talked a while; His plane was called and I gave him a smile

He got up to leave, and then he said; "You know, it's too bad you aren't dead." I sat there a moment, then felt a shade, And I thought, "I guess there's no parade." On my flight home I thought of him,

And then wrote this on a whim:

Peace-nik, beat-nik, hippie and dove; mix together and add some love; boil it, and spoil it,
and send it to school;
and then forget the Golden Rule.

The following is true for any Vet returning from any war:
"We who have seen war . . . Will never stop seeing it. In the silence of the night, we will always hear the screams." —Joe Galloway *We Were Soldiers Once, and Young*

AFTERTHOUGHTS

LIFE IS COMPLICATED. I SPENT TWO-AND-A-HALF YEARS IN Nam as a medic, mostly as a Dustoff medic. I saw all the carnage man can do. I also saw how the politicians were hemming and hawing about the war. By the time I left, I was realizing that soldiers were winning battles but politicians were not trying to win the war. At that point I thought, *What the hell are we fighting for then? Take a hill, then give it up?*

I concluded that if the politicians don't want to win the war, then all the GIs getting wounded and killed would be a waste. A waste! I turned against the war when I got home but I didn't turn against the soldiers fighting it. I turned against it because I didn't want to see any more guys get killed in battles the politicians didn't care about, or appreciate, or use to help win the war. If they didn't want to win, then fuck 'em. Why should our guys go over there and get killed for no reason?

After beginning to watch Ken Burns's Vietnam series in September 2017 (I could only watch about 20 minutes at a time, and never got past Episode 3), it is clear that the US made a lot of misjudgments and mistakes from the end of WWII until we finally got out.

As a Vietnam combat veteran, I feel alone. The war was wrong from the get-go and what we were *asked to do* was wrong, but what we *did* was not wrong. In battle, you are not fighting for your Country's policies, your Constitution, or for your loved ones back home; you are fighting just so you and your buddy can live.

We saw, we heard, we ducked, we cried, we hurt, we killed, we feared, and we died. Once the battle was over, we all knew those still breathing had our back. We had, and would, sacrifice ourselves to save the others. Like Shakespeare wrote in *Henry V*, we became a band of brothers. But the only part of the *Henry V* speech that belongs to us is: "We band of brothers."

On our return we were never welcomed, honored, or respected for what we did. We were blamed for the mistakes the politicians' made. On the day of my return, in the Seattle Airport, I was wished dead. But we have no shame for what we did, for what we did was for Country, Duty, and Honor. Though our belief in our government was abused, none of us want to dwell on that for very long.

For the past half century, we have found ourselves alone in the world—except for each other—but we retain our steadfast pride for having taken care of our brothers and for having been faithful in doing what our country asked us to do. Our only wish is for the politicians and citizens of this country to be worth dying for.

Larry Kipp (Photo by Crew Chief Tom Cash)

ACKNOWLEDGMENTS

I WANT TO THANK ALICE SULLIVAN FOR GETTING me organized and for her very generous editing skills. I thank my son, Mastin Kipp, for being there and for hauling me back to Vietnam, which formed the impetus for getting me to finish this very difficult to write remembrance. And I thank the Combat Veterans Peer Writing Group leaders Richard B. Kelly, MD; Dr. Joseph Bathanti; and my fellow combat veterans of the Writing Group: Carl Zipperer, Bruce Turek, Dan Poteet, Eric Heisler, Frederck Moore, Gary Odell, Gil Crowson, Harvey Gershen, Rick Roman, Steve Wilson, Tony Hogsed and Stephen Henderson for all their patience, suggestions and–most importantly—for all the things we never had to say to one another because we, each of us, already knew. Most importantly, I want to thank all my crew chiefs and Aircraft Commanders I flew with for keeping our Dustoffs flyable and on path. Finally, I thank the late CWO Randy Radigan for his understanding and patience in teaching me to crew correctly.

AFTER VIETNAM, LARRY KIPP WORKED AS AN IRONWORKER, a stonemason and as a horse fence builder as he worked on his advanced degrees in agriculture and entomology. He graduated with a Ph.D in Entomology from the University of Kansas, and went on to become a research field biologist and university professor. Along the way he married, became a father and spent thirty-five years caring for his disabled wife while being senior editor for a scientific journal. Larry now resides in the mountains of North Carolina.

www.hellgatepress.com

Made in the USA
Middletown, DE
09 May 2023

30304235R00146